The New York Book of Tea

❖ Where to Take Tea ❖
and
Buy Tea & Teaware

Second Edition

The New York Book of Tea

❖ Where to Take Tea ❖
and
Buy Tea & Teaware

Second Edition

Bo Niles & Veronica McNiff
with illustrations by Susan Colgan

❖

CITY & COMPANY
NEW YORK

Copyright © 1995, 1997 by Bo Niles and Veronica McNiff
Illustrations copyright © 1995, 1997 by Susan Colgan

Design by Stacie Chaiken and Heather Zschock

Library of Congress Cataloging-in-Publication Data
Niles, Bo.
The New York book of tea: where to take tea and buy tea & teaware/
Bo Niles & Veronica McNiff.—updated & expanded ed.
p. cm.
Includes index.
ISBN 1-885492-37-5
1. Restaurants—New York (State)—New York—Guidebooks. 2. Tea.
3. Tea making paraphernalia. I. McNiff, Veronica. II. Title.
TX907.3.N72N463 1997
647.95747'1—dc21   97-8247 CIP

Second Edition

Printed in the United States of America

City & Company
22 West 23rd Street
New York, NY 10010

NOTE TO READERS: All prices and hours listed herein
are subject to change. Please call to confirm.

CONTENTS

TEAROOMS & RESTAURANTS

JAPANESE & CHINESE TEAS

SHOPS & BOUTIQUES, continued

WHERE TO BUY TEA: RETAIL & MAIL-ORDER

A Civilized Sip

Taking tea is a convivial activity, a perfect way for friends to get together. And so it is with us. Sometimes it is just a cup brewed in each other's kitchen. Sometimes it is a stop-off at a tearoom close by. Sometimes it is a leisurely indulgence taken at a midtown hotel.

Tea, simply put, is an enigma. What other beverage, after all, makes you feel so utterly of the moment and, at the same time, gently invokes the past and offers you the future in its leaves? Simultaneously stimulating and soothing, tea both rejuvenates and relaxes the body and the soul. When you take tea, you replenish your energies and you engage in contemplation. Tea is a tonic.

So why do we take tea? For starters, we grew to know each other when our sons attended the same school. We live in the same neighborhood. We share common interests—and the same middle initial. T!

Loving tea as we do, it made sense to us to pull together a second edition of this book when it became apparent that some bright new places for tea and tea things were opening up around town. And so, of course, that gave us the chance to share even more cups of tea.

And that still suits us—to a T.

Bo Niles & Veronica McNiff

A Tradition of Tea

Afternoon Tea, like Christmas trees and Santa Claus, is a tradition that was invented in the Victorian era. Unlike High Tea, which was the meal the British working class returned to after a long day laboring at the factory, Afternoon Tea was a formal, aristocratic affectation that evolved as a genteel ritual punctuating the long interval between lunch and evening supper.

The Afternoon Tea encountered today in New York consists of the traditional three courses, which are usually served simultaneously on a tiered cake stand. The presentation of the entire Afternoon Tea menu allows nibblers to graze at their leisure, but tea takers typically follow the three-course menu. In a formal setup, tea is usually of the loose variety, not bagged. After selecting a tea, the brewing tea and hot water are brought out separately, but in matching pots, perhaps with a tea cozy to keep the tea itself warm. The hot water is replenished at least once during the tea. If you ask for an infusion, you will get herbal tea.

The first course is comprised of a medley of finger sandwiches made from whole wheat bread, white bread, or a specialty such as pumpernickel bread, cut into bite-sized crustless rounds or rectangles. Traditional fillings include peeled, sliced cucumber; de-stemmed watercress; egg salad; sliced white chicken; and perhaps salmon, shrimp, or rare beef. Some menus try to dazzle you with more inventive fillings, or with relishes to spice up the basics.

The second course is usually a scone or two (depending upon whether it is a mega- or a mini-version), accompanied by so-called Devonshire cream—a thick whipped cream—plus a choice of preserves and marmalade. The third course is sweet: petits fours, tartlets filled with lemon curd or berries mixed in custard, miniature éclairs, and a cookie or two.

The traditional three-course Afternoon Tea followed by most of the hotels we went to may be offered at a prix fixe, or à la carte. The à la carte menu tends to be more ample and includes fruit, or a selection of cakes. Some places offer both kinds of service; if so, they typically add a selection of sparkling wines, sherries, and ports to the line-up. Indeed, some hotels like to have you segue into the cocktail hour.

Although teatime, in the British tradition, is a four o'clock rite, most venues in the city have taken liberty with the time frame. Some begin offering tea right after lunch; others, in fact, serve tea virtually all day long. Hotels will take reservations, particularly on weekends and during the holidays. Most of the other venues listed herein are more casual and will simply seat you when you arrive; if you do not want to take a chance, telephone ahead to see if a reservation is necessary.

Where to Take Tea

Tea is the most welcoming and accommodating of beverages. It can be enjoyed virtually anywhere, be it at home, on the run, or in one of the lovely spots around town dedicated to its service. In New York, the delights of taking tea are as many and myriad as are the venues where tea is offered. A formal, traditional Afternoon Tea, with its three-course menu comprising sandwiches, scones, and sweets, can be indulged in with the approriate fanfare and flourishes at more than a dozen of the city's most prestigious hotels. Because visitors to the city who might request or expect tea tend to gravitate to the grander hotels that cluster in the midtown area, hotel teas reflect this penchant. Tearooms, by contrast, which are genially eccentric by nature, tend to be tucked away in casual, out-of-the-mainstream spots their owners have taken a fancy to. The twin lures of neighborhood and neighborliness are part of their distinctive and cozy appeal. Japanese and Chinese teas offer a tranquil alternative. Finally, department stores and museums are visited because their cafes do a brisk business in the afternoon when snacking revives flagging energies, and this implies a bracing cuppa, even if it is bagged.

Hotel Teas

The Palm Court at the Plaza

THE ASTOR COURT AT THE ST. REGIS

2 E. 55th St. bet. Madison and Fifth Aves. ❖ 753-4500

Hours: Daily 3 P.M. to 5:30 P.M.

Raised on a balustraded dias just inside the front door of the St. Regis, the Astor Court appears to be suspended under a pale, frothy sky, which is encircled by a mythological mural, painted by Zhou Shu Liang, depicting the Greek ideals of peace, harmony, and beauty. In colors of white, gold, and pink, it is as confectionary in spirit as the three-course tea it offers each afternoon. The Court's dozen or so tables cluster around a central statue banked by flowers. Table settings are exquisite: linens from Porthault and porcelain from Limoges, by way of Tiffany & Company, are designs exclusive to the hotel. Tea—black, herbal, or scented (eighteen choices in total)—is presented in silver teapots to the soothing strains of a harp or a piano. Rock candy sugar sticks, both amber and crystalline, to dip into your tea at whim, add a sweet touch. Champagne, port wines, sherries, eau-de-vie, and dessert wines are also offered for an additional price. If something stronger is desired, proceed into the King Cole Bar, and, while there, take in the famous Maxfield Parrish painting of the slightly dyspeptic king.

Price: prix fixe, $29

THE COCKTAIL TERRACE
AT THE WALDORF-ASTORIA

301 Park Ave. bet. 49th and 50th Sts.   ❖   872-4818

Hours: Daily 3 P.M. to 5:30 P.M.

Long a magnet for presidents and proletariat alike, the Waldorf-Astoria sits proudly upon a patch of New York turf just south of St. Bartholomew's Church and a half dozen blocks north of Grand Central Station. Tea service, formerly held in the Peacock Alley alcove, has recently moved to a more spacious lounge overlooking the west end of the lobby. Elevated above the lobby's hum of visitors and walk-through pedestrians, the Terrace is a genial oasis in which to enjoy a pot of Darjeeling and a triumvirate of nibbles: scone, mini-sandwich, and pastry. Islands of cushy seating are well-spaced on the luxurious carpet; huge square columns and a gilt rail further increase the feeling of privacy. At the appropriate time, a piano player situated in the middle of the space signals a segue into the cocktail hour. Four additional tables poised at the corners of the mosaic floor on the lobby level allow people-watchers to sip and speculate at their leisure.

Prices: prix fixe, $20; with a glass of sparkling wine, $29

FITZERS AT THE FITZPATRICK

687 Lexington Ave. bet. 56th and 57th Sts.   ❖   355-0100
Hours: Daily 3 P.M. to 5:30 P.M.

A quiet enclave of Gaelic charm unexpectedly close to the bustle of 57th Street, this is the New York outpost of a family-owned Irish hotel chain. Everyone working here is as Irish and as friendly and disarming as any soul you might care to meet in County Clare. Make a right off the lobby, where the *Irish Echo* and *Irish Voice* lie next to visitors' guides, to find Fitzers Restaurant. Tables are covered with emerald green tablecloths, surrounded by pink and green tapestry-clad French chairs with a moss-green carpet underfoot. The teatime experience is more like a country hotel tea than a genteel citified four o'clock. The teapot contains two teabags as big as baby pillows; a trio of warm, currant scones come with butter and a huge dollop of strawberry jam. On one visit, two Englishmen nearby tucked into it all with gusto while doing business.

Prices: Irish High Tea, $12; Light Tea, $7; pot of tea for one, $2; basket of scones with butter and jam, $3.50

THE GALLERY AT THE CARLYLE
35 E. 76th St. at Madison Ave.   ❖   744-1600
Hours: Daily 3 P.M. to 5:30 P.M.

Finding the Gallery is a bit of an adventure as neither of the two entrances into the Carlyle suggest its presence. Your best bet is to access the hotel from its Madison Avenue entrance and proceed up steps, past the Carlyle Cafe and Bemelman's Bar (pause to peek in at the delicious murals by the illustrator of the beloved Madeline books). Voilà! The Gallery is really an intimate anteroom to the hotel restaurant. With just five tables, a miscellany of kilim-covered sofas of various pedigrees and inclinations, and fringe-trimmed fire-red velvet highback chairs, the Gallery exudes an air of mystery and suspense. The intense mood lighting also adds to the Gallery's mystical ambience. The near-dizzying riot of patterns in the miniscule space is relieved by the jewel-toned palette. One almost expects to be offered a hookah rather than a serious tea, and, as a matter of fact, some of the clientele appear to be anticipating just that. Thick accents and intense hunching over papers is often the modus operandi here. It is as far from the madding crowd as you can get! Next stop: the souk.

Prices: prix fixe, $22.50; pot of tea, $5; à la carte tea sandwiches, $11; scones, $9.50; and miniature pastries, $9

THE GARDEN CAFE AT THE HOTEL KITANO

40 E. 38th St. bet. Park and Madison Aves.   ❖   885-7000

Hours: Daily 3 P.M. to 5 P.M.

What a surprise. The Kitano offers not one, but four afternoon tea menus in its spacious Garden Cafe. As you walk through the main lobby, pause to growl back at the Botero sculpture of a dog. The Cafe, a few steps down from the rear of the lobby, is a lofty, naturally lit atrium space with ficus trees. Warm cherrywood panels enclose the walls; the tables and vaguely Biedermeier chairs are solid but graceful; and a large and colorful original tapestry hangs on the west wall. In all, an attractive ambiance that makes you feel cosseted in a world-traveler kind of way. The dainty traditional Afternoon Tea is an excellent standard. But there's also Chocolate Delight, and à la carte tea service. The chocolate option includes: your choice of Godiva Hot Chocolate, Chocolate Almond Tea, or Raspberry Coffee, accompanied by finger sandwiches, tea cakes with chocolate whipped cream, and Leonidas chocolates, pralines, and cremes. If Peach Apricot Tea is your thing, then Fruit Explosion will please. Afternoon Spirits adds a choice of liqueurs. Service is gracefully efficient, as befits the value the Japanese set on manners both private and public.

Prices: set teas, $15.50 to $18.50; pot of tea, $3; miniature pastries, $7

THE GOTHAM LOUNGE AT THE PENINSULA
700 Fifth Ave. at 55th St.   ❖   247-2200
Hours: Daily 2:30 P.M. to 5 P.M.

Just steps up from the entrance hall, on the way to the reception area, the Gotham Lounge is a hushed sanctuary, both for hotel guests and for visitors strolling in from shopping or a matinee. Three huge arched windows look out to the chocolate walls of the Fifth Avenue Presbyterian Church. Decorated in a peaceful manner and in the palette of a men's club, with walls painted to simulate a tawny-hued stone, the Lounge embraces a panoply of unmatched tables and chairs, all calculated to coddle, whether you are alone, with a companion, or with a group. Rosy velvet club chairs, tapestry-clad French-style fauteuils, and ruddy-toned wooden chairs with a slight art nouveau flair pull up to tables which are accented with flowers and bowls of nuts. Of the teas served, three are Twinings and eight are from Jacksons of Piccadilly, including Jasmine and three herbal blends. In addition to its mini sweets, the menu offers an aptly titled Five Cake Temptation. The Gotham Lounge is also a bar, so a full complement of spirits, ports, and sherries are available either during tea, or after. Taped music purrs softly in the background.

Prices: prix fixe, $25; Canton Delicate Ginger, $8; glass of champagne, $12.50

ISTANA AT THE NEW YORK PALACE
455 Madison Ave. bet. 50th and 51st Sts.   ❖   303-6032
Hours: Daily 3 P.M. to 5:30 P.M.

It's a little early to tell how the Tapas Tea, newly introduced by the Palace's Istana restaurant, will fare. Still, it's certainly worth a visit. As you enter the imposing courtyard of what was once the Villard Mansion you understand why the name was selected. It's quite grand inside, too, if a bit over-gilded and glitzy. There is a vaguely Moorish feeling to the architecture, reinforced by a richly red carpet of swirling arabesques and red velvet banquettes with squashy pillows. Red velvet cartouches on the wall display Spanish-looking plates; butter-yellow tablecloths match the lighting emitted by myriad brass sconces and chandeliers. The Tapas Tea menu is entertaining. First, try the Mediterranean Tea Sandwiches which include a lemon-cured salmon with zatar and a Spanish tortilla. Now you're ready for homemade burnt orange scones with cardamom creme fraiche; next, pastries. A selection of nine teas includes an excellent but powerful Lapsing Souchong (ask for hot water on the side in order to dilute the taste). Finally, have a glass of Alvear Pale Cream Sherry. Tapas Tea? It's a fun idea.

Prices: prix fixe, $25

LADY MENDL'S TEA SALON
AT THE INN AT IRVING PLACE

56 Irving Pl. bet. 15th and 16th Sts.   ❖   533-4466

Hours: Wednesday through Sunday 3 P.M. and 4:30 P.M.

This is a really delightful addition to the New York tea scene, named after one of New York's most redoubtable women, the seminal decorator Elsie de Wolfe, who, upon her marriage, became Lady Mendl. Would Elsie approve of this tea salon? Definitely. Eclectic vintage Victorian furnishings and tea things are displayed with artful aplomb. It's all very genteel: conversation is a discreet hum; quiet classical music is in the air. Go light on lunch and prepare yourself for *five* tea courses. First comes a little taste of fresh seasonal fruits; then a trio of mini-sandwiches; and next a plain or cranberry scone furbished with cream and preserves. This is followed by an offering of sweets and candied citrus peels, and finally, there's an over-generous slice of dacquoise. Choose your tea from a daily selection culled from a stock of thirty, including herbals. Summer brings iced teas, like White Peach. Note: The front stoop is a challenge to climb. But worth it.

Prices: prix fixe, $25

THE LOBBY AT THE ALGONQUIN
59 W. 44th St. bet. Fifth and Sixth Aves.   ❖   840-6800
Hours: Daily 11:30 A.M. to 4:30 P.M.

To partake of tea at the Algonquin, or 'Gonk,' is to sample something of American literary and theatrical history though, alas, the hotel does not offer a teatime menu as such. Still, it is worth a visit for its sense of place. The Algonquin opened its doors in 1902, attracting personalities such as Douglas Fairbanks, Sr., Gertrude Stein, and Eudora Welty. After World War I, Dorothy Parker, Robert Benchley, and other critics and writers started the Round Table, where over lunch they passed witty judgment on each other and the cultural events of the day. Within the hotel's cozy, oak-panelled lobby, where Twinings tea and various sweets may be ordered, it always feels like afternoon; the one window is obscured by a swath of velvet, and there's ever a glow of lamplight. An assemblage of squashy velvet sofas, tufted leather chesterfields, upholstered armchairs, and well-used copper-topped tables invite you to be seated; fresh flowers spring from posh old Oriental vases. All is mellow, suggesting a clubby atmosphere of long duration.

Prices: pot of tea, $3; tranche of fruit tart or pie, $7

THE LOBBY AT THE ROYALTON

44 W. 44th St. bet. Fifth and Sixth Aves.   ❖   869-4400

Hours: Monday through Friday and Sunday 3 P.M. to 1 A.M.;
Saturday 3 P.M. to 2 A.M.

The Algonquin and the Royalton face off across 44th Street in one of those New York style-standoffs that makes the city tingle. The Algonquin represents the small, distinguished old hotel tradition; the Royalton is where the new chic crowd of rock stars, top magazine editors, wealthy wannabes, and YBAs (young/beautiful/ambitious of any gender) congregate; the Philippe Starck designed environment will surely be landmarked around 2050. The gray slate lobby is luxurious in an extraterrestial, underground sort of way. Starck stretched the long narrow bi-level space even further with a bright blue runway of carpeting which is detailed with Dr. Seuss-like motifs. Tea is served to you as you're seated in oversized Jetson-style seats wrapped in white tie-on napery. While you wait, surreptiously eye new arrivals as they parade down Starck's catwalk.

Prices: pot of tea, $4; plate of cookies and savories, $6

THE LOBBY LOUNGE AT THE FOUR SEASONS
57 E. 57th St. bet. Madison and Park Aves. ❖ 758-5700
Hours: Daily 3 P.M. to 5 P.M.

The Four Seasons Hotel, located between Madison and Park Avenues, is one of Manhattan's most recent entries on the hotel scene. The breathtakingly lofty, but austere, lobby of pale stone is visually softened by a carpeted and mirrored balcony where tea is served. The narrow space holds just a handful of tables, sinuous velvet sofas plumped with enormous pillows, and sink-into chairs that encourage lingering. Both black and oolong teas are offered, as well as a trio of aromatic herbals—rose hips, peppermint, and chamomile. The tea menu is sensibly apportioned according to cravings: a traditional three-course Afternoon Tea, with an optional glass of sherry; finger sandwiches, with a tall flute of sparkling wine, if desired; or two freshly baked scones, accompanied, if you wish, by a vintage port.

Prices: prix fixe, $24

MARK'S AT THE MARK
25 E. 77th St. at Madison Ave.   ❖   744-4300
Hours: Daily 3 P.M. to 5:30 P.M.

With its matte-polished paneled walls decorated with framed prints of statuary in an array of poses, forest-green carpeting, and velvet-upholstered seating in shades of mustard, rose, and mulberry, the Mark exudes an old-world ambience perfectly suited to its pair of Afternoon Teas: The Mark Tea and The Strawberry Cream Tea. The variables to the two teas are the sweets. The Mark offers petite pastries in lieu of the strawberries and crème chantilly that are the main component of the tea by that name. Both teas feature a tea sandwich filled with Louisiana prawns, accented with roasted pepper relish. To reinforce the intimate, clubby mood, and to create pools of privacy, Mark's is laid out on three levels, which are punctuated by wrought iron railings, banquettes, columns, and the occasional potted palm. On the lower level, a mammoth floral arrangement girdled with tufted velvet seating takes center stage. Dress code here is casual, running the gamut from stilettos to tennis shoes. Tea may overlap with lunch because Mark's is the hotel's restaurant. The bar swings into action later in the day.

Prices: prix fixe, for both Afternoon Teas, $16.50

THE PALM COURT AT THE PLAZA
768 Fifth Ave. bet. 58th and 59th Sts. ❖ 759-3000
Hours: Monday through Saturday 3:45 P.M. to 6 P.M.;
Sunday 4 P.M. to 6 P.M.

The Plaza may be the Hollywood vision of what constitutes a grand hotel; it is done with aplomb and the best money can buy. And indeed a fringe of palms define the court, situated in the central lobby. They look as new and flourishing as the rest of the furnishings. There are acres of mirrors, massive marble columns, and plenty of bright gilding lavished on the giant caryatids and the lofty coffered ceiling, with its vast glittering crystal chandeliers. "Better than Fortnums!" exclaimed the Anglophile, lying replete in her comfortable red velvet chair after sampling the prix fixe tea. Service is impeccable; the tablecloth is crumbed between courses; the teapots are quietly checked for hot water; fresh flowers appear on the table as the blazered musicians launch into Mozart, and then *Les Miserables*. The Palm Court's own tea blend turns out to be Harney's, a Keemun black tea served piping hot and strong. Next: a tray selection of pastries made in the Plaza's own kitchens. A vast silver serving trolley displays all of the possiblities of the house pâtisserie to keep those waiting for a table in delicious torment.

Prices: prix fixe, $23; pot of tea, $4; tea sandwiches, $10; scones, $8.50; choice of cake or three miniature pastries, $8.50; glass of champagne, $12.50

THE PEMBROKE ROOM AT THE LOWELL
28 E. 63rd St. bet. Park and Madison Aves.   ❖   838-1400
Hours: Daily 3:30 P.M. to 6:30 P.M.

A room with no view, this hat-and-gloves dowager of tearooms turns quietly inward and focuses on the simple delight of taking tea without interruption or distraction. Swag and jabot window treatments in an appropriately tea-stained chintz and lace undercurtains camouflage the nonview, and tables are set with rosebud topiaries in faux verdigris terracotta pots. The tea trolley offers a dozen teas, which include standard blacks as well as a variety of infusions. The à la carte menu features English crumpets, fresh fruit and cheese, and, for the incipient sniffle, a hot toddy. Hot buttered rum and a concoction known as the East India Company Cocktail are also on the list. The only difficulty here is one of access: the Pembroke Room is discreetly located on the second floor of the hotel, and you virtually have to genuflect to locate the correct elevator button.

Prices: prix fixe, $21.50; pot of tea or an infusion, $4; à la carte menu, from $8 to $18.50; hot toddy, hot buttered rum, or East India Company Cocktail, all $7

THE ROTONDA AT THE PIERRE
2 E. 61st St. at Fifth Ave.   ❖   838-8000
Hours: Daily 3 P.M. to 5:30 P.M.

Enormous murals with a mythological bent encircle this aptly named space furnished with eight tables for tea. Trompe l'oeil society dames strut across a faux-balustraded walk. Satyrs, nymphs, and other assorted types leer and peer from behind monumental columns and revelers and gamblers frolic through a pastorale that seems to mate *A Midsummer Night's Dream* with the oeuvre of some junior apostle in Tiepolo's workshop. The clientele is similarly eclectic: a grandmum, mum, and daughter are prettily poised; a May-December duo are contemplating their next move; beyond, two young things are comparing muscle tone. The traditional tea may be complemented, for a surcharge, with a sparkling wine or with a sherry. Goodies are also available à la carte.

Prices: prix fixe, $26; Tea and Bubbly accompanied by sparkling wine, $34; Fino Tea paired with sherry, $34; à la carte treats, from $11 to $14

Tearooms & Restaurants

ANGLERS & WRITERS

420 Hudson St. at St. Luke's Pl.   ❖   675-0810

Hours: Monday through Saturday 9 A.M. to Midnight; Sunday
10 A.M. to 11 P.M.; tea service, daily 3 P.M. to 7 P.M.

Anglers & Writers could be a home away from home for Ratty, the
philosophical rodent fisherman of Kenneth Grahame's *The Wind in
the Willows*. As it is, many of the city's downtown literary denizens
find this a most compatible spot in which to hang out, meet their editors, or restfully read someone else's book over a pot of tea or a glass
of wine and an omelette. On Sundays, it is packed. If you get the
round table right of the entrance, you will have a wonderful view of
the Hudson River. More water notes: creels, lures, and well-used fishing rods and reels signify the contemplative art of angling. While you
await your tea, delve into one of the many well-used books on the
open shelves. Owner Craig Bero is from rural Wisconsin and on a
quiet afternoon, this place feels like you might find it in a small town
where the skies are big, the winter is long, and the snow is deep, and
no one has ever heard of Garrison Keillor. Bero's mother has a wonderful way with baked goods, and turns out toothsome wonders in the
kitchen. Try the marvelous fruit scones.

Prices: prix fixe, $12.50; glass of wine, $3.50; pot of tea, $2; dried
fruit scone with butter and jam, $1.75; slice of cake, $4.75;
pie, $4.25

THE BARNES & NOBLE CAFES

2289 Broadway bet. 82nd and 83rd Sts.   ❖   362-8835
1972 Broadway bet. 66th and 67th Sts.   ❖   595-6859
160 E. 54th St. bet. 3rd and Lexington Aves.   ❖   750-8033
675 Sixth Ave. bet. 21st and 22nd Sts.   ❖   727-1227
33 E. 17th St. bet. Broadway and Park Ave. So.   ❖   253-8080
4 Astor Pl. bet. Broadway and Lafayette St.   ❖   420-1322
Hours: Daily 9 A.M. to 11 P.M. or later

Tea and a good book just go together. The soft-sell Barnes & Noble attitude towards books works wonders with squooshy sofas and armchairs plus big tables and robust library-style chairs which encourage browsing. The atmosphere in both is at once relaxed and studious: students brush elbows with young mothers with kiddies in tow. Check out the neo-deco photomurals of famous writers in curious combinations: Faulkner sips with Steinbeck and T. S. Eliot; Carl Sandburg hunkers down with Edith Wharton; Hardy with Emily Dickinson. Bagged tea is from The Republic of Tea and Bigelow. Inventive sandwiches are offered, as well as cakes by the slice and giant cookies. Barnes & Noble also presents adult and children's book readings, signings, and poetry events.

Prices: cup of tea, $1; sandwiches from $1.50 to $4.50; cookies from $1.25; cake by the slice from $1.75; individual fruit tart, $2.25

CIII

103 Waverly Pl. at McDougal St. ❖ 254-1200

Hours: Tuesday through Saturday 7:30 A.M. to 10:30 P.M.;
tea service, 3:30 P.M. to 5 P.M.; closed Sunday and Monday

The restaurant CIII's name is actually the street number translated into Roman numerals—a nice scholarly touch for this Washington Square neighborhood, dominated as it is by New York University. Together, owner Judy Paul and chef Charles Simmons have devised a menu based on new ideas about American foods, with a grace note drawn from French cuisine. Paul, whose parents own the Washington Square Hotel which shelters CIII, added a tea menu a couple of years ago. On fall and spring Saturdays, the restaurant offers walking tours exploring the Village; these popular explorations culminate with tea at CIII. The restaurant's exterior is modest; you step down into the space itself from the sidewalk. Inside, there are sturdy mahogany tables and serviceable chairs. Select the day's Tea Sampler, a prix fixe menu which lets you choose from one of about a dozen black leaf teas, and six herbal brews. The finger sandwiches may include tarragon gravlax on black bread, or smoked turkey with cheddar on sourdough. Scones are offered, along with fruit butters. Sweets may include brownies, or something special to the day (all baking is done in house). You may also compose your own à la carte version of teatime.

Prices: prix fixe for one, $6.95; for two, $12.95

DANAL

90 E. 10 St. bet. Third and Fourth Aves. ❖ 982-6930
Hours: Tuesday through Sunday 10 A.M. to 10 P.M.; tea service,
Friday and Saturday 4 P.M. to 5:30 P.M.; reservations required;
closed Monday.

Tucked into a nondescript block on the fringes of the wholesale
antiques district, Danal is a country place redolent of a summer some-
where between the English shires and the south of France. The kitchen
area is right up front, its blue-tiled counters piled high with huge bowls
of fresh vegetables and fruits. While you sip your tea, watch the kitchen
staff prepare and bake one of their many delectables; delicious oven
aromas float on the air, along with a thread of music. Take your place
at any one of the old pine tables—in all shapes and sizes—which are
matched up with eccentric chairs or rumpled pillow-tossed loveseats.
Everything is faded, clean, and friendly with use. Teapots new and old
are cupboard-stored in full view, as is the Mottahedeh china, a repro-
duction of an 1820 Staffordshire pattern. Tea goodies show up as
hearty crust-on sandwich breads to nutmeg-scented, currant-studded
scones, and buttery cakes. A dance card-sized handwritten menu with
a flowered cover itemizes five unblended and two decaf black teas; an
oolong and two green teas plus seventeen thés aromatiques and four
herbal infusions. Danal also sells these loose from a nook by the door.

Prices: prix fixe, $14

E.A.T.

1064 Madison Ave. bet. 80th and 81st Sts.   ❖   772-0022

Hours: Daily 7 A.M. to 10 P.M.

Teatime at this genial Upper East Side to-go/stay-in combo bistro alludes to a special afternoon menu that makes the most of the establishment's fabulous bakery goods, which range from a sumptuous chocolate cupcake to a yummy, overscaled, perfectly proportioned linzer torte or shortbread heart. The tea selection, despite the menu's title, is spartan—just the standard bagged English and Irish Breakfasts, Earl Grey and Darjeeling, plus Chamomile. But who cares, when you can indulge your sweet tooth and hang out as you wish? E.A.T., with its mirrored walls and checked floor, bespeaks an industrial efficiency that perfectly suits Madison Avenue mothers. During the interval between naptime and the presupper screamies, little Jennifer and Jason can drip and drool from their strollers, and it can all be wiped up.

Prices: cup of tea, $2; sweets, $2 to $6

EDGAR'S CAFE

255 W. 84th St. bet. Broadway and West End Ave. ❖ 496-6126
Hours: Sunday through Thursday 11 A.M. to 1 A.M.; Friday and
Saturday 11 A.M. to 2 A.M.

The Edgar referred to here is actually Edgar Allan Poe, who wrote
The Raven nearby. In the poet's day, this was farmland. Now it is West
84th Street. Prepare yourself for a modest surprise on entering; it is
as if an Italian trattoria set up business in a sunny ancient Roman ruin,
after doing a few twenty-first-century renovations with modern elements such as metal mesh and modern lighting. In fact, the interior
was designed by an architect from Florence, a friend of the two owners, both of whom hail from sweet-toothed Mediterranean cultures that
enjoy the social art of lingering over good food; hence the relaxed
ambience. With twenty-six small marble tables and wrought iron chairs
packed into this cavernous space, it can be a little noisy later in the
evening, but the atmosphere is convivial. There is no prix fixe tea, but
Twinings black and fruit-flavored teas are served all day, as are semoli-
na roll sandwiches. Incredibly, there are eighty varieties of cake to sample (twelve are chocolate), some imported by air from Italy.

Prices: tranche of cake, $4.25 to $4.95; cookies from $3.50 for a
quarter-of-a-pound; pot of tea, $1.50

KING'S CARRIAGE HOUSE

251 E. 82nd St. bet. Second and Third Aves.   ❖   734-5490
Hours: Daily 3 P.M. to 4 A.M., reservations required

When Elizabeth King met her future husband, Paul Farrell, in his native Ireland, she confessed to him that she'd love to replicate Irish manor-house hospitality in New York. Three years ago, the couple realized that dream, converting a former bookshop in a charming two-story brick carriage house into a place to lunch, dine, and take tea. Their traditional Afternoon Tea is served under the languid gaze of three antlered stags in the sunny yellow Willow Room overlooking a slip of a garden. Here a hot pot of Irish-blend leaf tea is accompanied by comfy cucumber-padded triangles of crustless bread, salmon on toast and curried chicken tartlets, miniature scones with jam, and a tempting array of tiny sweets. Liz and Paul showcase a bi-annual boutique during the Christmas holidays and in April where they sell Irish linens, teas, and assorted treasures collected on trips home to Ireland and England. Teapots, from J. Sadler, march in a tidy row across an Irish scrubbed pine hutch. The upstairs Red and mural-embellished Hunt Rooms, seating 28 and 16 respectively, are available for private teas; bridal showers are particularly popular.

Price: prix fixe, $16; crown-topped and cottage-shaped teapots, $52

LE PAIN QUOTIDIEN

1131 Madison Ave. bet. 84th and 85th Sts. ❖ 327-4900

Hours: Daily 8 A.M. to 7 P.M.

Museum-goers will be happy to discover Le Pain Quotidien—it's just a few steps away from the Met and Museum Mile. Be warned, though: it's already a favorite of its Upper East Side denizens, who appreciate its relaxed ambiance, peach-smudged walls, and sleek blond wood interior. So you may have to wait for a spot at the 20-ft.-long communal table up front; or opt instead for one of the tables at the back. In fact, everything—down to the last perfectly tailored fixture and marble-and-chrome shelf—hails from Belgium. Tondos of crusty loaves, glazed and gleaming patisseries, Belgian chocolate, jams, spreads, olive products such as tapenade, and six to eight imported teas are sold to take away, as is a caffeine-free fruit tisane. The locally-baked breads are made from imported flour, patisserie is made on the premises. It's fun to stay for tea: your individual pot comes with a long-handled spoon-infuser so you can brew to your taste while you sample scrumptious sandwiches and bijou pastries, and eye the crowd.

Prices: pot of tea, $2.75; sandwiches $7.50 to $13; pastries and pies, $3.50 to $5

MACKENZIE-CHILDS, LTD.

824 Madison Ave. at 69th St. ❖ 570-6050
Hours: Monday through Saturday 10 A.M. to 6 P.M.

Ascend the twiggy stair to the top of this quirky emporium and you'll find yourself in the cozy rooms Victoria and Richard MacKenzie-Childs have set to celebrate their Sweet Tea. Tea here comes straight out of a storybook; this is no mere pot-and-bag production, but rather a delicious "presentation" worthy of the Mad Hatter and Co. Once settled at your table, a warm lavender-infused moist towel is brought to you in one of their charming covered butter dishes, along with a wee tartan-covered folder filled with painted-postcard renditions of the nearly two dozen presentations you can choose from. To the accompaniment of a player piano, the waiter draws a white glove over your free hand; this is your napkin. Among the presentations, one that stands out is the "cake decorating party" for two which includes, besides the cake, a panoply of sugar hearts, crystal sugars and the like, and a pair of tweezers so you can execute your handiwork with delicacy and aplomb. The actual teas served are three: Earl Grey, Mint, and Light Rose.

Prices: Presentations $38 per person; cake decorating party for two, $38 per person; a sampling of all the home-made sweets, with tea, for two, three, or four, $64.

PÂTISSERIE LES FRIANDISES

972 Lexington Ave. bet. 70th and 71st Sts. ❖ 988-1616

Hours: Monday through Saturday 8 A.M. to 7 P.M.; Sundays
10 A.M. to 6 P.M.

When Les Friandises opens its doors each morning, the golden smell
of butter and baking perfumes the entire block. A tiny, clean, all-white
space dominated by a French belle epoque poster, Les Friandises has
six miniature cafe tables and French country chairs with rush seats.
Prize-winning pastries, gateaux, tartes tatin, cookies, and tea delectables sell as fast as chef-owner Jean Kahn can make them, especially at the holidays. As likely French-speaking as English, customers for-
give the Twinings tea in paper cups, focusing instead on dainty
brioche sandwiches, followed by, say, the Desirée: a dense chocolate-
almond ganache atop a thin layer of chocolate cake, glazed with
chocolate, finished with a piped design and candied violets.
Irresistible. Try the Chocolate Rum Chestnut Cake, too.

Prices: container of tea, 75¢; brioche tea sandwiches, $2 each; tea
and dessert pastries from $1.50 to $4.15; cake portions from
$3.75; 6-inch cakes from $10.50 to $21

PAYARD PATISSERIE & BISTRO

1032 Lexington Ave. bet. 73rd and 74th Sts.   ❖   717-5252

Hours: Daily 7 A.M. to 10 P.M.; tea service 3 P.M. to 5 P.M.

The eagerly anticipated Payard, named for award-winning pastry chef Francois Payard, has emerged, like a phoenix, from a graffiti-scarred storefront on an antiques-and-bookstore swath of Lexington Avenue. Together with his partner, four-star restaurateur Daniel Boulud, Payard had created what must be every Francophile's fantasy of the Parisian patisserie. Just inside the front door you'll find pastry cases filled with every sinful indulgence you ever dreamt of—from tiny truffles to extravagances such as the dozen fanciful confections named for the most famous monuments and chateaux in France. Payard is tidily divided into three comfortable, chocolate-and-buttercream-hued spaces: the entry shelters a lively coffee-liquor bar, which leads into a sumptuous banquette-lined dining area uplifted with a mezzanine. We sank into our three-course "Thé" in one of the corner banquettes. Nearby, well-behaved children sipped Payard's delectably rich hot chocolate. Payard's special tea is a lemon/bergamot-infused blend.

Prices: Le Thé, $14.50; Le Tea Royal, with caviar and blini $19.50; pot of tea, $5

SANT AMBROEUS

1000 Madison Ave. bet. 77th and 78th Sts. ❖ 570-2211

Hours: Monday through Saturday 9:30 A.M. to 10:30 P.M.; Sunday 10:30 A.M. to 6 P.M.; tea service, daily 3:30 P.M. to 5:30 P.M.

The little konditorei of Yorkville, where once plump, well-tailored Viennese and German matrons gathered over cream-filled pastries, pampered dachshunds lolling at their neatly shod feet, are long gone. But Sant Ambroeus keeps a chic, Italianate version of this continental tradition alive. Walk past the seductive Italian ice creams up front, past the stand-up bar where strong espresso and apéritifs are dispensed, and by the glass cases where pastries are displayed like jewels, to find the tea salon at back. Coziness prevails in the art-deco inspired manner preferred by German-speaking patrons, who tend to elegance, blond hair, and serious diamond rings. French, Italian, and Spanish nationals also congregate to mingle with well-heeled Upper East Siders of an afternoon. White damask covered tables are set far enough apart to suggest privacy but mandate sampling conversations on either side. Select from three black tea blends or three herbal sachets; panini; and share your generous portion of Chocolate Cake Sant Ambroeus with a friend. Embellished with shavings of chocolate, rosettes of chocolate icing, bursting with airy chocolate mousse, it is self-indulgence perfected.

Prices: pot of tea, $4; panini, $4; pastries, $1 to $4.50; glass of champagne, $7

SARABETH'S KITCHEN

1295 Madison Ave. bet. 92nd and 93rd Sts.   ❖   410-7335
423 Amsterdam Ave. bet. 80th and 81st Sts.   ❖   496-6920
Hours: Monday through Friday 8 A.M. to 10:30 P.M.; Saturday
9 A.M. to 11 P.M.; Sunday 10 A.M. to 10 P.M.

New Yorkers are divided as to which Sarabeth's they prefer—though it is not a matter of taste, per se, since the same Sarabeth comfort foods—lemon cake, pumpkin muffins, oatmeal, milk-and-cookie plates, and preserves (which grownups just eat by the fruity, palate-piquant spoonful) are available at either location. If you head for the Sarabeth's on Madison, you will notice it is a little more dressed up to suit this cachet neighborhood, with its boutiques and Corner Bookstore (one of the last bastions of adventurous literacy in the city). The Madison Avenue Sarabeth's is full of tapestry-clad banquettes, flowers in baskets, brass chandeliers, and a vast two-story paned glass window that makes you feel as if you are inside a giant dollhouse. The West Side Sarabeth's is more informal with white-painted wainscotted walls. Order from the desserts/teatime menu.

Prices: pot of Twinings, $2; cake with whipped cream and strawberry, $5; muffin with dollop of jam, $2; milk and cookie plate, $6

T SALON & TEA EMPORIUM

11 E. 20 St. bet. Broadway and Fifth Ave.   ❖   358-0506

Daily 10 A.M. to 10 P.M.

As we go to press, the new T Salon is a work in progress. When proprietor Miriam Novalle removed T from its huge, former venue under the SoHo Guggenheim to its new digs in a three-story building in the Flatiron District, she promised a reincarnation, but it's been slow going. The familiar leaf-strewn velvety banquettes are in place, snuggled at the corners of the ground floor tea room which embraces a dozen tables and a tea bar featuring plump scones and a selection of teas. The look is vaguely Mackintosh with a soupçon of Art Nouveau thrown in for good measure. Up a flight of high-tech metal stairs, the emporium is highlighted by a wall of tea canisters and by a long counter displaying an eclectic assortment of tea things old and new plus the odd book and notecard. Teas from Mariage Frères as well as T's own blends are available for purchase.

Prices: pot of tea with scone: $7.25

TEA & SYMPATHY

108 Greenwich Ave. bet. Seventh and Eighth Aves. ❖ 807-8329

Hours: Monday through Friday 11:30 A.M. to 10 P.M.; Saturday and Sunday 10 A.M. to 10 P.M.; tea service, Monday through Friday 11:30 A.M. to 6 P.M.; Saturday and Sunday 1 P.M. to 6 P.M.

If your average lovable British mum opened a tearoom, this might be it. Ten tables with strawberry-printed oil cloths are squeezed into this tiny space; there are pictures of royalty, and an impromptu collection of bulldog pictures pasted right onto the painted walls. The menu speaks from the heart with British fare such as baked beans on toast, scotch eggs, hot Bovril. There is Sunday dinner (lunch to you) with roast beef and Yorkshire pud, at least until the food runs out, the waitress disarmingly confides. In summer, there is iced tea. Ask them to add Ribena, a black currant syrup much in favor over there. They even sell Tizer, a fizzy orange drink popular in the 1950s. When English patrons slide in for their cuppa, they request toast with Marmite, held to be a sure cure for homesickness. Ordering the cream tea, a West Country specialty, means scones with real clotted cream: thick, sticky, and delicious.

Prices: Afternoon Tea, $14; scones, cream, and jam, $4.25; Cream Tea, $5; pot of tea, $2

TELEPHONE BAR & GRILL

149 Second Ave. bet. 9th and 10th Sts.   ❖   529-5000
Hours: Daily 11:30 A.M. to 2 A.M.; lunch tea Monday through
Friday 11:30 A.M. to 4 P.M.

Three bright red cast–iron English phone boxes mark the East Village
facade of this cheerful, publike hangout a few steps below street level.
What is more, you can use them. Inside there is a low-ceilinged warm
glow through which you will distinguish a large bar long on imported
beers, battered wood floors, exposed brick walls, and to the right,
tables overlooked by large naïve paintings of generic nineteenth-century scenes. Brits nostalgic for high tea, a very different phenomenon
from ladylike Afternoon Tea, head right here. Airline crews, visiting
actors, and English models know the Telephone will give them a 'cuppa char' all day, along with a plate of bangers and mash, fish and
chips, or shepherd's pie. It is the kind of stodge that keeps the British
workman going; but you can also order a more genteel "lunch tea"
with finger sandwiches and sweets. Telephone caters private affairs in
the shoe-boxy backroom; one wedding tea for forty included tea sandwiches, buttered crumpets, and currant orange scones, served on pretty, mismatched plates collected by the friendly manager and chef.
Summer service is ad hoc—check ahead of time.

Prices: lunch tea, $8.95; pot of tea, $2.00

TROIS JEAN

154 E. 79th St. bet. Lexington and Third Aves.   ❖   988-4858
Hours: Monday through Saturday 11 A.M. to 11 P.M.; Sunday Noon
to 10:30 P.M.; tea service, daily 2:30 P.M. to 5:30 P.M.

For Francophiles, visiting Trois Jean may be the next best thing to
hopping the Concorde to Paris, so quintessentially Gallic is this elegant but friendly little bistro, a plus-chic version of Dalloyau, the ven-
erable Parisian tea salon haunted by that city's chic and wellborn. In
New York, they come here. Signals from the street tell you you are
leaving Manhattan behind: the clipped potted trees, the discreet window with Trois Jean emblazoned on it, a semiotic valance of lace
above. When you push the door open, your eye is immediately en-
tranced by the mouthwatering appearance of the gleaming, be-fruited
and chocolate-curled pâtisseries which are made fresh daily and presented in the glass fronted case. Crisply clothed tables are arranged
facing a long banquette, and fresh flowers bedeck the massive
mahogany bar—everything is fresh and spotless, even the long aprons
of the young French waiters. It all induces a pleasant sense of culinary
expectation that will be gratified at lunch, tea, or dinner. Trois Jean's
menu describes fifteen Mariage Frères teas served for "le four
o'clock." You choose your own pastry. Mmm!

Prices: pot of tea, $4; pastries $3 to $6.50

YAFFA'S TEA ROOM

353 Greenwich St. at Harrison St. ❖ 966-0577

Hours: Monday through Saturday, 2:30 P.M. to 5 P.M., reservations required.

Yaffa's Tea Room has its own entrance on Harrison Street, or it can be entered through Yaffa's original venture, a quirky neighborhood bistro bar on the corner of Greenwich Street. The tearoom menu varies daily. One day, the savory might include puff pastry wrapped around grilled vegetables, cucumber finger sandwiches, or grilled goat cheese in scented oil. Then maybe there are warm lemon-ginger scones with marmalade and butter, and next a selection from the redoubtable dessert menu. Slivers of pear tarte tatin, chocolate truffle cake, or tiramisù, for example, are presented together like flower petals on a plate. There are thirty loose teas that can be brewed at your request, ranging from three kinds of lemon and jasmine teas, to Moroccan peppermint tea, to ginger, to rose hip, as well as that old stalwart, Earl Grey. Yaffa is proud of the tearoom's wainscoted interior with its high tin ceiling; she spent months combing flea markets for the eclectic furnishings and finds that compose the fanciful decor. The brick wall has a fresco, and the artwork adorning the walls sometimes includes canvases by painter friends. Velvet curtains, mismatched wrought-iron tables, tapestry-clad chairs, and thrift-shop chandeliers dispel the gritty reality of the Tribeca streetscape just outside the window.

Prices: prix fixe, $15; glass of port or champagne, $6 and up

Japanese & Chinese Teas

THE FELISSIMO TEA ROOM

10 W. 56th St. bet. Fifth and Sixth Aves.   ❖   247-5656
Hours: Tea Service, daily 3 P.M. to 5 P.M.

An idiosyncratic and environmentally-conscious space, the Tea Room and Artspace on the top floor of this beaux arts limestone townhouse turned home shop features a "Haiku" menu at the set teatime. Trendy Downtown designer Clodagh outfitted the room with craftsy cherry wood tables: ovals for two, rounds for four, rectangles along the velvet-upholstered L-shaped banquette that can serve a huddle. A rubbed metal bar displays the teas in tins, over two dozen of them, from the California-based Republic of Tea. Tea is poured into diminutive black stoneware pots set upon matte-finished tiles, with hand-thrown, handle-less cups and napkins rolled in Felissimo's signature twig-and-cord tie ups placed alongside. Lovely, big, almost translucent Osenbei cookies with citrus imprints, a nut-encrusted cake, and scones are a sampling of the accompaniments. Nice touch: a rack of newspapers for browsing. There is no sense of rush here at all. Check the schedule for gallery openings or performances to enhance your stay.

Prices: "Haiku" tea, $16; small pot of tea, $2.75; large pot, $5; Osenbei cookies, $2.75 for three

41

KELLEY AND PING

127 Greene St. bet. Prince and Houston Sts.   ❖   228-1212

Hours: Daily 11:30 A.M. to 11 P.M.

The front of this self-styled Asian grocery and noodle shop at the Houston Street end of gallery-and-boutique lined Greene Street is devoted to tea—both to its sale and sipping. One entire wall is lined with shelves housing enormous canisters that dispense two dozen teas, whose very names might inspire poetic indulgences: Iron Goddess of Mercy, Gen Mai Cha, Gunpowder, and Chrysanthemum are just a sampling. Teas in tins—Spice, Lotus, Lemon, and Vanilla—and accoutrements, such as clay teapots and bowls, are displayed upon a shelf just behind the two tables and toadstool perches where tea can be taken—along with mooncakes from Taiwan, egg custard tarts or coconut tarts, and assorted small cookies.

Prices: pot of tea, $2; mooncake, $1.75

THE TEA BOX AT TAKASHIMAYA

693 Fifth Ave. bet. 54th and 55th Sts.   ❖   350-0100

Hours: Monday through Saturday 3 P.M. to 5 P.M.; closed Sunday

Descending to the lower level of this Japanese department store is like sliding into a tranquil pool—it is so serene and enfolding. Elevator doors whisper open to an anteroom devoted to the presentation of teas and tea things (see page 84). Beyond a low wall are two tearooms, each a study in the interplay of gentle geometries and the soft neutral tones of sand and stone. The rear room, a sanctuary of calm, is ringed with banquettes banked with soft, linen-clad pillows, and lit by tiny mesh-encased halogen bulbs. A luncheon menu segues seamlessly into the Afternoon Tea, which features The Tea Set, a pot of tea (there are thirty-seven to choose from), accompanied by a trio of exquisite cookies, either butter-based by West and Yoku Moku, or Vegetable by Suetomi. An East-West Afternoon Tea includes fresh fruit and Bernachon chocolates flown in from Lyons. An à la carte menu is also available.

Prices: The Tea Set, $6.50; East-West Afternoon Tea, $14.50

TEN REN TEA AND GINSENG COMPANY
75 Mott St. bet. Bayard and Elizabeth Sts. ❖ 349-2286
Hours: Daily 10 A.M. to 8:30 P.M.

This glittering, streamlined emporium is a branch of a Taiwan-based corporation, where many of the teas served and sold are grown; others are from China. As you walk in, you will be poured a tiny cup of golden-hued green tea, which you can sip as you scan the meticulously organized interior. Twenty varieties of black, oolong, and green teas are sold here. The finest quality teas are Tung Ting Oolong and Pouchong Green Tea; there are six grades of each from which to select. There is a tea-tasting table at the rear, where calligraphy and a wall painting set the mood, as does a selection of contemporary teaware. This is where free courses in tea tasting are held. Ten Ren also sells Taiwanese-style tea sets, with very small teapots made both by individual potters and by mass production methods. If you want to learn more about their teas and brewing technique, just pick up one of the many helpful brochures offered.

Prices: tea from $7.20 to $130, per pound (sold in 1-oz. increments); tea sets up to $900

TORAYA

17 East 71st St. bet. Fifth and Madison Aves.   ❖   861-1700
Hours: Monday through Saturday 11 A.M. to 5:30 P.M.; Thursday
11 A.M. to 6 P.M.; closed Sunday

Occupying the ground floor of a townhouse off Madison Avenue,
Toraya is a magnet for visiting Japanese who want to partake of their
native wagashi, a confection the Japanese consider an enticement for
all five senses and the perfect companion to their delicate, native
green tea. Toraya's tea shop, devoted to the presentation and sale of
boxed confections, is as tidily designed as a tea chest, containing oak
cabinetry so finely crafted that the joinery appears virtually seamless.
The tearoom itself, located in the back, feels like an architectural ren-
dition of a minimalist haiku. Soft, diffused light spills in upon the two-
story atriumlike space through an arched, coffered sandblasted glass
skylight and tall casement-style windows. Colors in the room—rose,
salmon, rust, celadon, teal, and stone—are the same hues as many of
the delicacies on the menu. Banquettes covered in watered silk line up
along the walls and face leather chairs of Italian design across the two
rows of tables. Despite uncovered marble inlay floors, conversation is
muted.

Prices: cup of tea, $2.50; wagashi, $4

Department Store Teas

Le Salon de Thé at Henri Bendel

CAFE ON 5IVE AT BERGDORF GOODMAN

754 Fifth Ave. bet. 57th and 58th Sts.   ❖   753-7300

Hours: Monday through Wednesday, 11 A.M. to 5 P.M.; Thursday through Saturday, 11 A.M. to 7 P.M.

A hum of contented conversation permeates this elegant space, with its Neo-Italian ambience. The travertine marble is the color and visual texture of nougat, there are suave black table tops, and squooshy black leather banquettes, and a small bar from which the beverages are deftly dispensed. The wait staff, like all of Bergdorf's personnel, seem to exemplify what the last word in bodily and fashionable self-presentation ought to be. There are no decorative elements at all, unless you count the large, ebullient sunflower plates, pinwheeling with manic Van Gogh vivacity on the walls. The real decoration is the food. Generously portioned, the provender is brilliantly colored. The polenta is a vivid marigold yellow, the peppers red hot red, the salad green as emeralds. The clientele, smartly turned out in their ultra chic outfits, look equally radiant as the foodstuffs. So much for lunch: the prix fixe tea is certainly up to scratch, too. A different selection of sandwiches is offered daily—smoked salmon, rosemary chicken mousse—and five kinds of black or herbal tea. Cookie plates may include shortbread, biscotti, or chocolate chunk, delicious morsels all.

Prices: prix fixe, $12; plate of cookies, $5

CAFE SFA AT SAKS FIFTH AVENUE

611 Fifth Ave. bet. 49th and 50th Sts. ❖ 753-4000

Hours: Monday through Saturday 11 A.M. to 5 P.M.; Thursday until 7 P.M.; Sunday 12 P.M. to 5 P.M. Tea menu, Monday through Friday 3 P.M. to 5 P.M.

Yes! Saks now offers a prix fixe tea menu. The luxury store would not want you to faint half way through your shopping day from sheer hunger, and so it created Cafe SFA for judicious breaks for elevenses, lunch, and tea. The Cafe environment is bold, blond, and Biedermeier, with oversized architectural elements. Tapestry-clad chairs draw up to clothed tables; yellow-scumbled walls give off a sunny glow. The perimeter loggia offers skyline views, particularly one corner which overlooks St. Patricks Cathedral. The tea rises to the setting. Your repast arrives on a tiered stand. Begin with assorted tea sandwiches and move on to a crumbly home-made scone and a muffin with lemon curd, Devonshire Cream and Spoon Fruits preserves. Nibble gourmet cookies as you sip your choice of tea. The Special Grade Keemun is a nice change from Earl Grey, or choose the Silver Tip Jasmine Yin Hao if you are feeling very ladylike. China Gunpowder Temple of Heaven is a handrolled green tea; there are also three flavored teas, and three herbal tisanes. If it's getting late in the day, you may wish to order a glass of fruity Mondavi Moscato d'Oro to go with the dulcet strains of the harpist.

Prices: prix fixe, $18.50; glass of Moscato d'Oro, $6.75

PARLOUR CAFE AT ABC CARPET & HOME
888 Broadway at 19th St. ❖ 473-3000

Hours: Monday through Friday 10 A.M. to 8 P.M.; Saturday, 10 A.M. to 7 P.M.; Sunday 11 A.M. to 6:30 P.M.

The Parlour Cafe epitomizes ABC's Victorian kitsch/decayed palazzo take on design. Rosy exposed brick walls are anchored by ruddy-toned Oriental rugs scattered on the wood floor. Eccentric unmatched tables and chairs nudge each other for elbow room in the warm gloom lit by candles. Above your head, exposed wood joists and metal ductwork jostle with heavily swaged drapes and funky sparkly chandeliers, while much-carved armoires and mock-majestic mirrors create a welcoming glamour. There's a bar counter, and beyond it, an open kitchen (it's always fun to see bustle when you're relaxing). The tiny square tea menu offers two choices: The Parlour Tea is a pot of tea of choice with warmed scones, deliciously crumbly and lavished with preserves and creme fraiche. There's also Chinese Jasmine green tea, Lime Sencha green tea, and Big Ben, a black tea made in the up-front English style. The Classic Tea option includes the Parlour Tea menu but with tea sandwiches and miniature fruit tarts and cookies so demure you can't believe they'll hurt your diet.

Prices: Classic Tea, $12; Parlour Tea $6

LE SALON DE THÉ AT HENRI BENDEL

712 Fifth Ave. bet. 55th and 56th Sts.   ❖   247-1100

Hours: Tea Service, daily 2:30 P.M. to 5 P.M.

Backlit by the glorious frosted Lalique windows facing Fifth Avenue, Le Salon de Thé offers a scintillating overlook from which to view Bendel's brown-and-white striped shopping bags bob through the store. To distinguish the tearoom, gilded or painted cubes project from the wall; each cube is a pedestal for an insouciant teapot. Cozily scaled tables emblazoned with squiggly lines are hugged by chairs upholstered in stripes; each table is centered with a single, perfect rose in a sleek deco-style vase. Afternoon Tea—also known as Après-Midi à Bendel—is offered prix fixe, with or without a flute of bubbly. There is a full menu for Petit Dejeuner, Coupes Glacées, Boissons Chauds and Froids, plus a separate wine list. What a charming way to brush up on your "français." Le Salon de Thé, located at the second level of the atrium, can be reached by stairs or elevator.

Prices: prix fixe, $14, with champagne, $19.50; cup of tea or iced tea, $3.50; pâtisserie, $5; coupe glacée, $6.50

LE TRAIN BLEU AT BLOOMINGDALE'S
1000 Third Ave. bet. 59th and 60th Sts. ❖ 705-2100
Hours: Tea Service, Monday through Friday 3 P.M. to 5 P.M.

Le Train Bleu describes itself as a nostalgic re-creation of a luxurious French railroad dining car. Indeed, as you sit in green velvet-upholstered and carpeted comfort, surveying snowy white tabletops running the length of the handsome narrow mahogany interior with its mirrored railcar windows, you could almost swear you feel Le Train Bleu gently swaying over the tracks. A prix fixe tea is served on signature china by formally dressed waiters; six loose teas are yours to choose from, served in old-fashioned hotel silver pots, strainers alongside. Tea sandwiches are of the smoked salmon ilk. Wolfgang, the manager, confides that the day's pastries sometimes include apple strudel "because I'm Austrian." No wonder Le Train Bleu's cosmopolitan charm is a world apart from the bright white universe of housewares that prefigures this hidden oasis at the back of the sixth floor.

Prices: prix fixe, including a glass of sherry, $12.50

Museum Teas

T, Salon • Restaurant • Tea Emporium
Below the Soho Guggenheim

THE GARDEN CAFE
AT THE MUSEUM OF MODERN ART

11 W. 53rd St. bet. Fifth and Sixth Aves. ❖ 708-9400

Hours: Saturday through Tuesday 11 A.M. to 5 P.M.; Thursday and Friday Noon to 8 P.M.; closed Wednesday

The atmosphere in the ground level cafe, which takes a long view into and through the birches that grace the museum's sculpture garden, is vaguely redolent of a European railway waiting room. With glue-on arched mirrors, globe lights, walls stained shoe-polish brown, and terrazzo floors, the space does not pretend to be great design, but it is comfortable. Woven bistro chairs give the cafe just the right touch of color. Food is served cafeteria-style to keep everyone moving, including knapsacked students, glassy-eyed tourists scanning their maps, and office workers in for a bite on their break. Teas, all bagged basics, are perfunctorily displayed alongside the cash registers at checkout, so you must fill a cup with water ahead of time. Sweets and baked goods—croissants, brownies, muffins, and the like—are the usual lineup, but there is also a selection of desserts, including tiramisù.

Prices: cup of tea, $1; sweets, $1.75; tiramisù, $3.50

THE MORGAN COURT
AT THE PIERPONT MORGAN LIBRARY

29 E. 36th St. at Madison Ave. ❖ 685-0008

Hours: Tuesday through Friday 11 A.M. to 4 P.M.; Saturday 11 A.M. to 5 P.M.; Sunday Noon to 5 P.M.; tea menu, Tuesday through Saturday 2 P.M. to 4 P.M.; Sunday 2 P.M. to 5 P.M.; closed Monday

When the Morgan Library decided to connect its companion brownstones, it did so with a soaring skylighted atrium designed by the Manhattan-based firm Voorsanger & Associates. A gridded metal-and-glass ceiling rises wavelike over a quartet of black olive trees, and pale stone walls acurl with bleeding hearts and ivies. It is a glorious feeling to step into this airy link after the studied dimness of the mansions. Tables covered in an Americana green check linen are spotted about the marble floor. It is here that one can stop and enjoy a traditional three-course tea, or an à la carte cuppa after viewing a current exhibit or paying respect to J. P.'s book room and Renaissance-style library, or after paying a visit to the gift shop across the way. The à la carte menu features a gingerbread recipe culled from the family archives as well as sandwiches, scones, and cookies.

Prices: Afternoon Tea, $15; pot of tea, $1.75; Louisa Morgan's Gingerbread with whipped cream, $3.25; tea sandwiches, $6.50; scone, $2.50; cookies, $3.50

THE MUSEUM BAR ℘ CAFE
AT THE METROPOLITAN MUSEUM OF ART

1000 Fifth Ave. at 82nd St.   ❖   535-7710

Hours: Tuesday through Thursday and Sunday 11:30 A.M. to 4:30 P.M.; Friday and Saturday 11:30 A.M. to 8:30 P.M.; closed Monday

The Metropolitan's combined eateries—Restaurant, Cafeteria, and the Bar ℘ Cafe—are entered via the long hall devoted to Greek and Roman antiquities. The skylit restaurant and cafe are set off by sprightly new grey-and-white-striped, scalloped awnings, and two charming, loosely hung, painted canvas murals depicting fashionable ladies out for a stroll. The Metropolitan allocates quick bites, tea, and beverages to a cozy corner just inside and to the right of the entrance to the restaurant. A dozen round tables draped with black tablecloths and an art deco mural over the bar stand out within the cavernous, vaulted, and colonnaded two-story-high space. Efficient, courteous service guarantees a pleasurable respite from the rigors of checking out the incredible wealth of treasures found in the Metropolitan. A traditional Afternoon Tea service, offered throughout the day, features tea sandwiches and scones, plus an assortment of cakes and pastries.

Prices: tea, $2; scone, $4.50

THE MUSEUM CAFE AT THE GUGGENHEIM

1071 Fifth Ave. bet. 88th and 89th Sts.   ❖   427-5682
Hours: Sunday through Wednesday 9 A.M. to 6 P.M.; Thursday
9 A.M. to 3 P.M.; Friday and Saturday 9 A.M. to 8 P.M.;
closed Monday

Tucked under Frank Lloyd Wright's cantilevered coil, the Museum
Cafe can be accessed both from Fifth Avenue at 88th Street, and
from the museum proper. The cafe's twenty black granite-topped
tables sit upon industrial gray carpeting. A series of portholes set into
the exterior wall allows pinhole peeping from the sidewalk. To inspire
small talk, the exterior wall and the wall at the back of the cafe are
blanketed from the chair rail to the ceiling with oak-framed pho-
tographs documenting the museum and luminaries associated with its
history, including Wright himself in his signature hat and cape. Bagged
tea is served in glass mugs throughout the day, along with a selection
of fresh-baked goodies, including muffins and brownies that can be
picked up, cafeteria-style, from a sleek-brushed steel counter running
virtually the entire length of the cafe. A special treat is the moist and
chewy lemon curd cake.

Prices: mug of tea, $1.25

SARABETH'S RESTAURANT
AT THE WHITNEY MUSEUM OF AMERICAN ART

945 Madison Ave. bet. 75th and 76th Sts. ❖ 570-3670

Hours: Tuesday Noon to 3:30 P.M.; Wednesday through Friday 11:30 A.M. to 4:30 P.M.; Saturday and Sunday, brunch menu, 10 A.M. to 4:30 P.M.; closed Monday

At the base of Marcel Breuer's upended brutalist ziggurat and behind a two-story facade of glass is Sarabeth's, a full-service eatery where bagged tea is always at the boil, and a dessert menu is primed to sweeten the palate. The two dozen white-clothed tables, modernistic tapestry-clad and vaguely ergonomic chairs and robust ironstone are positioned upon the slate floor with enough space between them to ensure a restful ambience for catching up on buzzwords and bon mots as well as on the elusive pleasures of the Biennales, both here and abroad. On the way out, stop off and refresh yourself with the ingenuous ingenuity of Calder's Circus at the top of the stairs.

Prices: cup of tea, $1.75; dessert, $6

Where to Buy Teaware

The search for teaware gives purpose to endless happy prowling through country antique shops, city flea markets, and neighborhood tag sales. You never know where teaware or lovely linens for your table may turn up.

Between us, your authors own sixteen teapots, countless cups, saucers, and mugs, several sets of dessert plates, numerous cake stands, and myriad odd but attractive bread, cookie, and cake plates, all of which were purchased with pleasure and are fondly brought out at a moment's notice.

Today the style and conventional equipage of an elegant Afternoon Tea is still much as it was in the time of Queen Victoria, when the right wares were considered essential to the enjoyment of the moment. Following are descriptions of the tea furnishings and accoutrements you might expect to find in an English country house, circa 1900. It is fun to collect any or all of these or to create your own style of tea presentation.

Setting the Table

Teapoy: a small pedestal table, often mahogany, with a lidded compartment to hold glass or lead containers for tea, and glass porcelain mixing bowls for combining special blends.

Tea caddy: a container for tea made of silver, glass, porcelain, or rare inlaid wood in an extraordinary variety of droll shapes and sizes.

Caddy spoon: a short-handled scalloped spoon used to measure tea leaves. In the early days, Chinese merchants included a scallop shell tea leaf scoop in each chest of tea they shipped to Europe.

Mote spoon: a dainty, slightly pointed spoon with a shallow or pierced bowl. It is used to skim off specks of tea leaf, which can sometimes escape from the pot into the cup.

Tea strainer: a filter designed to catch tea leaves as tea is poured into a cup. Some strainers rest over the top of the cup; others affix to the spout of the teapot, swinging over the cup as the pot is tipped to pour.

Tea kettle: Some kettles can be lifted off their metal stands, which are fitted with a burner; others are hinged to the stand so that the hostess can tip the kettle to fill the teapot. Furniture makers developed kettle stands for this apparatus.

Tea tray: A tea tray can be almost two feet in length; it is designed to hold a kettle on its stand, a teapot, a sugar canister, tea caddies, and a milk pitcher. Such a tray might have been fashioned from solid silver, tole, or papier-mâché. Usually a tray is footed to prevent contact with wood surfaces; raised edges prevent things from sliding off.

Tea table: a small table, usually mahogany, with a carved or metal rim on which to place tea cups, spoons, and assorted tea foods. Craftsmen lavished their artistry and grace upon such tables.

Muffin dish: Made out of silver, this has a hot-water liner and high-dome lid to keep muffins warm.

Muffineer: A muffineer resembles a large-scale domed pepper pot with a perforated decorative top. It is used to sprinkle cinnamon or sugar on toasted goodies.

Toasting fork: a long handled, two- or three-tined, spindly fork made out of wrought iron with a wooden handle. It was intended to hold a bread slice or crumpet at arms length over the open fire so that you did not get your face and hands burned.

Sugar basin: a basin used to hold pieces of sugar broken off from a cone. (You can still find sugar sold in heavy cones.) Sugar tongs then permitted guests to pick up their sugar and drop it into the cup.

Slop bowl: a bowl in which to pour the dregs of the prior cup of tea.

Teacup: a shallow, gently swelling bowl with a single handle, from which tea is sipped. Some teacups are also footed. When the first handleless tea bowls arrived from the Orient, European ladies found them extremely uncomfortable to hold in the hand. By the mid-1750s, teacups with handles appeared.

Saucer: a shallow plate with a circular indentation into which is set the teacup. The saucer also has a shallow lip to prevent the cup from slipping off, and acts as an impromptu spoon rest. It was once considered acceptable to pour your tea into the saucer and sip it—some elderly British folk still do so.

Creamer: a small pitcher for milk, either matching the tea china, or of silver or other metal. The name is a misnomer, since cream should never be put in tea—its high fat content masks the flavor and oil globules may float on top.

Teaspoon: a pointed or oval spoon used for blending milk and dissolving sugar into tea. Decorative, shallow-bowled, oval teaspoons usually come in sets of six, eight, or twelve—or they might form part of a complete cutlery service. In the hierarchy of spoons, they come after the dessert and before the coffee spoon. The Victorians enjoyed novelty and souvenir teaspoons. Today teaspoons can be collected one-by-one to make amusing mismatched sets.

Shops & Boutiques

Myers of Keswick

ABC CARPET & HOME

888 Broadway at 19th St.   ❖   473-3000
Hours: Monday and Thursday 10 A.M. to 8 P.M.; Tuesday,
Wednesday, Friday, and Saturday 10 A.M. to 7 P.M.; Sunday
11 A.M. to 6:30 P.M.

ABC Carpet & Home is a phenomenon: This whole building devoted to the home is worth a visit even if you don't want to buy the superb Mariage Frères teas and tea accoutrements sold here. The store recently expanded into the building next door to create a table-top empire with myriad lines of china, cutlery, crystal, glass, and the like. Now the vast first floor is a glittering, furbelowed maze of mini-shops ranging from style concepts—Eastern Spirit, the Fifties Kitchen, and Theda Bara's boudoir—to specifics like plants, kids' clothes, and posh desk accessories for the executive. ABC's style of decorating marries Miss Havisham off to the Collier Brothers—the sheer abundance of merchandise and the festively over-the-top displays are like nothing else the city offers. The Mariage Frères boutique offers a full range of the long-established French company's tea in tins and gift packages; there is also Mariage Frère's own teaware—china, caddy spoons—cookies, and tea-flavored jellies. ABC also carries other tea accoutrements of its own choosing.

ADRIEN LINFORD
927 Madison Ave. bet. 73rd and 74th Sts.   ❖   628-4500
ADRIEN LINFORD ESSENTIALS
1339 Madison Ave. bet. 93rd and 94th Sts.   ❖   426-1500
Hours: Daily 11 A.M. to 7 P.M.

Adrien Linford started ten years ago as a single store on upper Madison Avenue; now there are two. Both are airy spaces full of extremely elegant accessories for bed, table and bath as well as a selection of gift books. The stores' signature shiny purple wrapping paper, tied with brilliant yellow or green ribbon, is a give-away signal to lucky recipients that something special has been selected for them. Linford is a good place to search out unusual serving pieces and tea time accoutrements, such as brightly colored painterly teapots and mugs, splashed with fruits and veggies, by Massachusetts potters Droll Design. In fact, about one-third of all of Linford's wares come from American artisans. That said, there's a kind of West Coast gestalt about these shops, dense with dramatic, oversized pieces made of pottery, rich woods, and glass, displayed in suggested table settings.

AGES PAST

450 E. 78th St. bet. York and First Aves.   ❖   628-0725

Hours: Monday through Saturday 11 A.M. to 5 P.M., but call ahead

A tiny clapboard nineteenth-century shopfront suggests a Connecticut seafaring town—Stonington, possibly. Inside, Ages Past is a repository of gentle nineteenth-century charm of the most rarefied kind: brilliant yellow canary ware, pink lustre, early Wedgwood, early to mid-Victorian English china. This is the place to discover transfer ware, too. In the eighteenth century, potters learned how to apply quaint and sometimes moral decorative scenes and mottos directly onto the china. While this may have been a technological novelty—or a way to save money—the resulting ceramics make charming tea collectibles, though you might want to save them for special occasions, like royalty coming to tea. In that case, Ages Past could assist you with commemorative tea things, a deft way to flatter a monarchical ego. These are a specialty here. Some of them are of very early time periods and correspondingly expensive but there are lots of affordable ones from the last two or three generations of Windsors.

BARDITH LTD.

901 Madison Ave. at 72nd St.   ❖   737-3775

31 E. 72nd St.   ❖   737-8660

Hours: Monday through Friday 11 A.M. to 5:30 P.M.

While waiting for the M2 Limited bus at 72nd Street and Madison, peruse the ravishing porcelains and other treasures visible through Bardith's windows. Inside, shelves and étagères are crammed with exquisite examples of the late seventeenth to mid-nineteenth century English, Continental, and Chinese porcelains, delft, faïence, and period glass. You may simply want to hold your breath with delight at their beauty, and terror lest you accidentally brush against something irreplaceable. Is it a coincidence that store personnel are slim and agile as eels? Bardith on Madison sells full-size and rare miniature teapots, partial tea sets, and single cups and saucers. The dozens of papier-mâché trays dating from the turn of the nineteenth century onward represent the city's best collection. Sequestered round the corner on East 72nd Street is a seraglio of complete tea sets. Scrolled in gold and indigo, lushly bouquet'd on gilt grounds, sprigged, dotted, striped, or swagged, these delicious creations require checks written with many zeros. Bardith also sells fine furnishings at this location.

BARNEYS CHELSEA PASSAGE

660 Madison Ave. bet. 60th and 61st Sts. ❖ 826-8900

Hours: Monday through Friday 10 A.M. to 8 P.M.; Saturday 10 A.M. to 7 P.M.; Sunday Noon to 6 P.M.

The Madison Avenue Barneys has devoted an entire floor to adorning the Manhattan home with objects and artifacts that represent the cutting edge in rarefied taste. This is where magazine editors cruise to see what's happening, and rising young movie stars dash in to shop for hot, new home furnishings before the photographer from the *Times* stops by to shoot them in their homes. Every conceivable style, it seems, has not only been anticipated but refined with that inimitable Barneys edge. A twenty-minute perambulation of the shop's table and tea things will send you out as dizzy and elated as if you had been in an orchid house too long. You may think you know exactly what you like before you go, but Barneys will show you one thing after another you would never have imagined you would crave, from antique to avant-garde.

BERGDORF GOODMAN

754 Fifth Ave. bet. 58th and 59th Sts. ❖ 753-7300

Hours: Monday through Saturday 10 A.M. to 6 P.M.; Thursday 10 A.M. to 8 P.M.

The epitome of luxurious chic, Bergdorf's seventh floor is Seventh Heaven for tea savant-collectors. Not only does the store sell tins of quality leaf under its own smartly designed label, it has dedicated an entire boutique to the service of tea. The only trick is locating it. Just like a whimsical shop from a fairy tale, it seems to move away as you advance through Bergdorf Goodman's enticing sequence of linked, lushly carpeted, richly stocked rooms. Decorated in well-bred tones of blonde, the rooms are a cornucopia of stylish accoutrements for the home, forming a glittering maze at the heart of which lies the Tea Shop. You would have to go far to find a better selection of distinguished antique, vintage, and retro teaware in one place—the painted charms of these period pieces are simply delightful. Everything is in perfect condition; not a chip anywhere. The old and older embroidered tea linens displayed on an antique stand look crisp and freshly laundered, as do the linen and lace tea cozies nestled in their basket.

BERNARDAUD

499 Park Ave. bet. 56th an 57th Sts.   ❖   371-4300

Hours: Monday through Friday 10 A.M. to 7 P.M.; Saturday 10 A.M. to 6 P.M.; closed Sunday

This elegant repository of French porcelains, which relocated from Madison to Park Avenue, has set aside an intimate boutique they call their salon de thé to showcase all things related to the service of tea. Amongst the panoply of wares, a glass teapot fitted with a silverplate infuser, a refined sterling silver toast rack, and a curvy caddy in Bernardaud's signature "Galerie Royale" pale jade and white stripe pattern stand out. Olivier Gagnere, the designer of the caddy—and myriad other teawares—masterminded the design of the shop as well, and it shows in telling details, such as the plushy sofas that invite the shopper (or the shopper's spouse) to linger awhile and enjoy the atmosphere. Bernardaud also carries a selection of ten leaf teas, including Ceylon O.P. Pettigalia, Verte a la Menthe, and caramel tea. These, too, are packaged in "Galerie Royale" tins. Bernardaud's own assortment of jams and condiments might be served in dainty little check-topped Limoges confiture containers. "Galerie Royale" boxed sets are also available: Check out the canister and tea package; it would make a lovely gift.

BE-SPECKLED TROUT
422 Hudson St. bet. Morton St. and St. Luke's Pl.   ❖   255-1421
Hours: Monday through Saturday 10 A.M. to 10 P.M.; Sunday 10 A.M.
to 7 P.M.

Packed to the gills with one of a kind finds from mittel Europa to the
icy reaches of northern Wisconsin, the Be-Speckled Trout is replete
with friendly and fanciful old tea things: antique tea cups and saucers
sold one by one to mix and match, arcane angling and fishing antiques
(flies hand-tied a generation ago in England are still pristine in their
maker's tin cases), jokey small novelties, and lodge-type souvenirs
easy on the pocket. The Trout is located next to Anglers ℛ Writers,
also owned by Craig Bero, and represents the owner's recollections of
his grandfather's general store back home in Algoma, Wisconsin. It is
a successful and charming distillation of those childhood memories.
Spied from the sidewalk, the modest, multipaned shop front reveals
elusive glimpses of teapots, each as distinctive a personality and shape
as village women gathered to gossip. Beyond, there is the promising
impression of Hoosier-style oak cabinets, crowded shelves, and glass-
fronted wooden counters laden with inviting objects. Baked goods
tempt from an old glass cabinet and there are Mariage Frères and
Harney ℛ Sons teas in tins or sold loose by weight.

CARDEL

621 Madison Ave. bet. 58th and 59th Sts. ❖ 753-8880

Hours: Monday through Saturday 9:30 A.M. to 6 P.M.

Cardel has offered fine china and porcelain to New Yorkers since 1867. For some time, the store was one of few in the United States that purveyed and took orders for heirloom quality Hungarian hand-painted and gilded Herend porcelain. Cardel offers fourteen Herend open stock designs such as the Meissenlike "Fruit and Flowers;" be prepared to wait up to eighteen months for Herend's spectacular special order patterns. In addition, Cardel sells or takes orders for Mottahedeh & Company's renowned reproductions of rare antique china (many derived from the company's own collections or those of American museums). Top of the line is "Duke of Gloucester," first made for the British nobleman circa 1770. It features twenty colors and is decorated with twenty-two karat pure gold.

FELISSIMO

10 W. 56th St. bet. Fifth and Sixth Aves. ❖ 247-5656

Hours: Monday through Saturday 10 A.M. to 6 P.M., except
Thursday 10 A.M. to 8 P.M.

Ascend the spiraling rococo stair within this renovated Beaux Arts
townhouse shop to its fourth floor and you will arrive at Felissimo's
Tea Room and Artspace. To complement teas from the California-
based Republic of Tea, which are sold by the tin, the shop presents a
small, but exquisitely selected, rotating display of Japanese clay and
stoneware teapots and bowls; the inventory changes with the artisan
and the season. The array is complemented by preserves and condiments, as well as by a few books. A more expansive inventory of table-
wares is presented on the floor below, where you will find linens, serving dishes, and other paraphernalia to enhance your tea setup.

FISHS EDDY

2176 Broadway at 77th St.   ❖   873-8819

889 Broadway bet. 18th and 19th Sts.   ❖   420-9020

Hours: Monday through Thursday 10 A.M. to 8 P.M.; Friday and
Saturday 10 A.M. to 9 P.M.; Sunday 11 A.M. to 7 P.M.

From the moment you walk into these packed-to-the-ceiling stores, you
know you are onto something different. Fishs Eddy carries industrial
china manufactured from the 1930s to the present day for diners,
country clubs, hotels, banks, and academic societies, supplemented by
their own generic versions. Funky one of a kind plates—from long-gone
restaurants, banks, and businesses you never heard off—decorate the
walls. Kitsch paintings from the 1950s, 1960s, and 1970s are
propped up here and there. Less is definitely not more as cups cas-
cade, plates teeter in piles, mugs, saucers, plates, butter dishes, pitchers, and creamers are piled in barrels crowded together on the plank
floor. The thick, friendly china that furnished America's childhood at
diners and family restaurants like the International House of Pancakes
and Mister Donut rubs alongside of the slightly more upscale restau-
rantware from sources such as the Hotel Dupont, The Houston Club,
and even The International Monetary Fund. Make yourself tea in
Fishs Eddy's diner-china teapots, then pour it into teaware from say,
the Royal Viking cruise ships, or Pan Am.

FORTUNOFF

681 Fifth Ave. bet. 53rd and 54th Sts.   ❖   758-6660
Hours: Monday and Thursday 10 A.M. to 7 P.M.; Tuesday,
Wednesday, Friday and Saturday 10 A.M. to 6 P.M.

Just up the street from New York's diamond market, Fortunoff's glitzy 1970s-style store is touted as a major resource for vintage estate teaware. Zip past banked trays of sparkling rings to find the elevator and take this to the fourth floor. Put on your dark glasses before stepping out onto the red carpet and slinking past the chromed pillars that hold up the soaring ceiling. The silvers, densely displayed on spotlit glass shelves backed with mirror, can only be described as staggering. The dozens of partial and full tea services on view may include trays; the style runs the gamut from robber-baron late Victoriana to Edwardian effete or Forties funky. Some of it is downright funny, some of it—like the chastely elegant signed George Jensen five-piece service, circa 1920, priced at $25,000—covetable.

JADE GARDEN ARTS & CRAFTS COMPANY
76 Mulberry St. at Canal St.   ❖   587-5685
Hours: Daily 10 A.M. to 7 P.M.

Jade Garden sells a plethora of latter-day Chinese arts and crafts, but the real reason to visit this shop is its selection of Yixing teaware. The ageless refined forms suggest the calm serenity of the infinite. Collectable Yixing 'violet sand' earthenware teapots are shaped from rarely occurring naturally colored clay deposits in a rural region of Northern China. The small sized pots are traditionally used for Yunnan teas, which are brewed very strong and served in tiny tea bowls. The potters of Yixing province still create refined, matte-glazed teapots in shapes that have not changed for centuries. The 'violet sand' fires to a variety of muted colors: violet-toned terracotta, taupes and leafbrowns, a green-tea hued olive tone, and various subtle blues in cerulean and indigo tints.

JAMES II GALLERIES LTD.

11 E. 57th St. bet. Fifth and Madison Aves. ❖ 355-7040

Hours: Monday through Friday 10 A.M. to 5:30 P.M.; Saturday
10:30 A.M. to 5 P.M; closed Sunday

Suitably located above the prestigious Hermès store on East 57th
Street, James II is a decorative arts collector's idea of paradise.
Owner Barbara Munves celebrates the nineteenth-century's delight in
confident color and pattern with verve and the two floors are packed
to bursting with finds for the well-dressed tea table. Precious things
include tea caddies galore, fashioned in Georgian cut glass, silver, sha-
green, and papier-mâché; sardine boxes (a feature of the fashionable
Victorian table); biscuit barrels; jampots; strainers; tea kettles large
and small, both silver and plated; full and partial tea sets; dessert
plates; and much, much more. Don't overlook the rare Victorian
miniature tea sets, or the 1930s metal-mounted ceramic tea trays and
extraordinary sandwich boxes handled like evening bags.

JAMES ROBINSON
480 Park Ave. at 58th St.   ❖   752-6166
Hours: Monday through Saturday 10 A.M. to 5 P.M.

James Robinson is just the place to go for a Georgian mote spoon—used to lift out the small tea leaves that sometimes shoot the teapot rapids into your cup. Restrained ideas about window display reaffirm its role as one of the city's most respected resources for Georgian silver, dazzling English and Continental dining and tea service porcelains (look for intact gilt), and antique jewelry. The firm's dignified persona and status is further expressed through its spacious Park Avenue premises decorously upholstered in library green, and punctuated with mahogany glass fronted cases. In these you will find sugar nippers, tea strainers, sugar casters, silver and glass jampots—all the antique accoutrements of civilized tea-drinking. Massive double doors at the rear of the store open to reveal a veritable silver vault, where teapots and coffeepots stand in serried ranks, along with tea caddies, cream jugs, and sugar bowls. If you are a connoisseur looking for a rare (and costly) octagonal George III teapot, start here. If you like and can afford very good tea things, James Robinson offers modern replicas, hand-hammered from a solid sheet of silver in the eighteenth-century manner.

LA TERRINE

1024 Lexington Ave. at 73rd St.   ❖   988-3366

Hours: Monday through Saturday 10:30 A.M. to 6 P.M.

Like a diorama of a nineteenth-century potter's shop, La Terrine's floor-to-ceiling shelving displays tightly packed, colorful ceramics. Everything you could ever want for the table can be seen at a glance from the sidewalk. Beautifully painted traditional artisan wares from Portugal, Italy, Brazil, and France crowd right up to the windows, pushing one another out of the way. Teapots with perky knobbed lids come in all shapes, patterns, and sizes; you can create full or partial sets item by item. If you cannot splurge right now, dodge around the massive columns that represent an obstacle course in maneuvering around the store, to award yourself just one of the individually painted mugs hanging from pegs. Natural wood walls and fixtures, paper packing "straw" cushioning the teetering piles of plates, and the cartons that always seem to have just been delivered from some continental point of origin, give La Terrine an informal feeling. There are stacks of vibrant Provençal and toile placemats and napkins to pillage, as well.

MACKENZIE-CHILDS, LTD.

824 Madison Ave. at 69th St.   ❖   570-6050

Hours: Monday through Saturday 10 A.M. to 6 P.M.

Strolling up the oh-too-chic and Euro-minimalist Mad Ave, the sprightly orange-striped, sawtoothed banner-awning of MacKenzie-Childs, Ltd.
comes as something of a shock. This piquant shop-cum-tearoom, replete
with comfy pottery and glasswares designed by Victoria and Richard
themselves, looks and feels like a cozy cross between Wonderland and
Oz. There's nothing at all Ltd. here, least of all the merchandise, which
fills every single square inch of the shop; frivolity reigns and you can
indulge any fairytale fantasy you desire. From tuffets to tassels to
teapots and cozies: you can mix and match to your heart's content to
create a fanciful table or tray for your tea. Teapots, mugs, cups and
bowls are stacked in quirky array everywhere you look; especially
appealing is MacKenzie-Childs' frill-edged checkered majolica in pretty
pastels. Check out their checkered teapot cookie, too, and the ecologi-
cally-correct brooch made from a pottery shard. And, if you drop in in
the afternoon, stay and enjoy their Sweet Tea.

MAYA SCHAPER CHEESE AND ANTIQUES
106 W. 69th St. bet. Columbus Ave. and Broadway ❖ 873-2100
Hours: Daily 10 A.M. to 8 P.M.

A fastidiously simple store where cheese from around the world peacefully coexists with culinary antiques and fine teas, Maya Schaper's is redolent of charm rather than brie. Schaper hunts down tea and dining wares on regular trips to Europe, carrying home with her as much as she can by hand. The exquisitely edited selection of antique and vintage wares, which date from about 1830 to 1940, change all the time and are displayed on old-fashioned wire shelving on your right as you enter the store. On any given day, expect to find old English Hovis brand bread pans; bread boards with wood-handled knives; complete and partial tea sets and dessert plates, painted, as was the ladylike fashion of the time, by Victorian women in need of an artistic hobby; cake stands; cut-glass jampots; and silver serving pieces and cutlery. In all, quite a culinary compendium. There are also attractively packaged teas for sale. At the back, and in the downstairs gallery, you will find old pine and painted furniture.

PIER 1 IMPORTS

1550 Third Ave. at 87th St. ❖ 987-1746
461 Fifth Ave. at 40th St. ❖ 447-1610
71 Fifth Ave. at 15th St. ❖ 206-1911

Hours: Monday through Friday 9 A.M. to 8 P.M.; Saturday 10 A.M. to 7 P.M.; Sunday 11 A.M. to 7 P.M.

With its sunny West Coast ways, Pier 1 is the perfect antidote to gray Manhattan blahs. The sprawling home furnishing and tabletop stores have an air of breezy cheer established by big windows, burnt-orange tile floors, and squared-off natural wood fixtures—étagères, stacking display units—that manage to evoke packing cases just prised open. Many of the artisan made offerings are exclusive to the Pier 1 chain and about 50 percent of the merchandise is new each year. There is always a generous array of informal tea things—mugs, Italian tea sets, and Chinese teapots and bowls, bamboo tea strainers, infusers, and even tea itself. It is currently sold by the half pound in a canvas tea bag emblazoned with a chubby stencilled teapot.

SARA INC.

952 Lexington Ave. bet. 69th and 70th Sts.   ❖   772-3243
Hours: Monday through Friday 11 A.M. to 7 P.M.; Saturday Noon
to 6 P.M.

Though it specializes in modern Japanese ceramics, Sara's contemplative aesthetic springs directly from Japan's ancient tradition of studied-but-spontaneous beauty in form and technique. (The name Sara is actually the Japanese term for dish.) In the window, glass, ceramic, and wood objects for partaking of tea or dining form a tranquil still-life composition. Inside the white shell of the store, table furnishings that range from brilliant-hued and playful to pure and ascetic repose on massive built in ledges. Owner Kumi Oniki directly imports ceramics from Japan, and most are exclusive to the store in this city. Two free-standing oak tables present table settings that combine Japanese forms with Western culinary requirements. Elegant 'furoshiki'—patterned cloths used in Japan for wrapping and carrying things—serve as napkins, placemats, or very special giftwrapping. Tea things abound for both Japanese and Western style service. While we visited, an American potter came in to talk over some of the new pieces with the manager. But if you glaze over at discussions of ceramic technique, submit instead to captivation at their effects.

TAKASHIMAYA NEW YORK

693 Fifth Ave. bet. 54th and 55th Sts. ❖ 350-0100

Hours: Monday through Saturday 10 A.M. to 6 P.M., except
Thursdays 10 A.M. to 8 P.M.; closed Sunday

Takashimaya is a sublime six-story repository of ultra-refined fashions
for the home and person, with a cross-cultural sensibility that embraces the best of Tokyo, Paris, and New York. Tea things are displayed with The Home Collection on the third floor, as well as in the
anteroom to The Tea Box on the lower level. The selection of Japanese teapots and bowls is complemented by lacquerware, linens, and
meticulously stitched leatherbound blank books and boxes. The few
conspicuous British-style tea things seem incongruous, but it must be
nice for some to know they are there, just in case they have a yen for
something in which to serve Earl Grey. A highlight of the lower level
is a footed tray, or tea box, which contains the elements—such as a
miniature bamboo whisk needed to whip up a froth on green tea—
which are essential to Chado, the tea ceremony. Smartly tailored,
paper-sheathed boxes behind the counter hoard loose teas that can be
purchased by the ounce.

WILLIAM-WAYNE & COMPANY

850 Lexington Ave. bet. 64th and 65th Sts. ❖ 288-9243
846 Lexington Ave. bet. 64th and 65th Sts. ❖ 737-8934
Hours: Monday through Saturday 10:30 A.M. to 6:30 P.M.
40 University Pl. at 9th St. ❖ 533-4711
Hours: Monday through Saturday 11 A.M. to 7 P.M.; Sunday
1 P.M. to 6 P.M.

William-Wayne's witty sensibility and eclectic mix of home accessories–along with the framed prints of impish monkeys always in res-
idence–guarantees the three stores (two are side-by-side) a place in the
city's pantheon of shopping resources. Stroll in to examine the charming displays, full of decorating ideas. Look for the antique teasets,
pretty mugs, Victorian cutlery such as bread forks and jam spoons–
and Victorian lemonade pitchers ideal for iced tea to create your
teatime setting. There are tea tables old and new, custom-made chairs,
and decorative pillows to sink back into with your cup of tea. Select
one of fifteen handsome open stock Limoges or Spode china patterns
for your bridal list (if you have it here, givers might get inspired).

WOLFMAN · GOLD & GOOD COMPANY

117 Mercer St. bet. Prince and Spring Sts.   ❖   431-1888
Hours: Monday through Saturday 11 A.M. to 6 P.M., except
Thursday 11 A.M. to 7 P.M.; Sunday Noon to 5 P.M.

Authors of *Great Settings* and *Forks, Knives, & Spoons*, Peri
Wolfman and Charles Gold know their tableware. The palette in their
spacious loft space in SoHo is basically monochromatic, highlighted
with silver and a few subtle, creamy earth and sea tones—seafoam,
acqua, ochre, and sand. If you like the idea of creating a cup collection, mixing and matching is a breeze here as the shop stocks literal-
ly dozens of styles of cups and saucers. To accessorize a setting,
Wolfman • Gold also carries teapots, milk pitchers, and various accoutrements such as strainers. The list goes on with linens, flatware, and
serving dishes. New to their stock of wares are big, warm-to-the-hand
mugs and bowls. Woldman • Gold also carries a range of overscaled,
sink-into sofas and armchairs, perfect for snuggling on an afternoon
with a cup of your favorite blend and a good book or video. And, PS:
check out their collection of birdhouses—they're charming.

Where to Buy Tea

Retail & Mail Order

There are a variety of places around town and elsewhere in the United States where you can purchase tea and teaware. (R) indicates retail sale. (MO) signifies mail-order service.

BALDUCCI'S (R) (MO)
424 Sixth Ave. bet. 9th and 10th Sts.
New York, NY 10011 ❖ (212) 673-2600
Hours: 7 A.M. to 8:30 P.M.; closed Thanksgiving, Christmas,
New Year's, and Easter

In the beginning, there was...Balducci's. This Greenwich Village bastion of fine foods has always held allure for its great range of products. Teas, however, are relegated to four shelves way in the back and the pickings are basic: a few Twinings and Royal Gardens; a few Wagner's, represented here most conspicuously by Ch'a Ching; and Grace Rare Tea taking up their own tidy shelf. All but the Grace Rares are bagged. Gift baskets are available by mail-order, so add one of the teas offered to your order.

R.C. BIGELOW (MO)
P.O. Box 3921; Milford, CT 86460 ❖ (800) 841-8158

The culmination of a meal at a good restaurant is frequently the prof-
fering of a Bigelow's Tea Chest—a shallow wooden box displaying the
company's tea bags (Constant Comment, Apple Orchard, etc.) to round
out your dining experience. The company has made these tea chests
and gift assortments available by mail order. Call for a brochure.

CHAIWALLA FINE AND RARE TEAS (MO)
The Ashley Falls Schoolhouse
P.O. Box 217; 21 Clayton Rd.
Ashley Falls, MA 01222 ❖ (413) 229-8088

Mary O'Brien opened the Chaiwalla Tea Room (One Main Street,
Salisbury, Connecticut), following a trip to India, where she became
enamored of tea. Today, she travels around the world to taste and to
select the teas she chooses to sell. In all, O'Brien sells eighteen teas,
including a limited number of leaf teas by mail order. If you want, she
will fax the mail-order form to you. Teas include two Darjeelings—one
from Marybong Garden, the other from Sungma Garden—which are
characterized by a muscatel flavor. Her Fine Green Hyson is the
green tea beloved of eighteenth-century Europe. Chaiwalla House Tea
is a milk tea with spices. A true tea lover, O'Brien has renovated a
nineteenth-century house in Ashley Falls, Massachusetts, where she
plans to open a tea learning center.

THE CHARLESTON TEA PLANTATION (R) (MO)
6617 Maybank Hwy.; Wadmalaw Island, SC 19487
(800) 443-5987, for tours, 803-559-0383

America's only native-grown tea, aptly named America's Classic Tea, is cultivated on an island that lies not far from the gracious city of Charleston. The plantation's first-flush tea, harvested in May and offered in a limited edition, is available while supplies last; other blends are offered year round. Harvest runs from May through October; daily tours, by appointment, can be taken during this time. Teas come bagged, loose, or packaged with jelly, honey, and/or wafers. Tea plants can also be purchased.

CORTI BROTHERS (R) (MO)
P.O. Box 191358; 5810 Folsom Blvd.
Sacramento, CA 95819 ❖ (916) 736-3800

Darrell Corti imports estate-produced oolong and white (traditional sun-dried-only) teas from Hong Kong tea merchant Wing-chi Ip, owner of the Lock Cha tea shops. The 'single-day harvest' teas are evaluated on site for their character to decide how long they should wither in the sun, be abraded in a rotating bamboo cylinder prior to fermentation, fired over charcoal, and rolled, kneaded and twisted by hand. The teas originate at the Zhang family tea garden in China's Fujian province, and are processed there by the proprietors. The oolongs are Golden Cassia, Hairy Crab, Tieguanyin; the white teas are Shoumei and

Fuding Silver Needle. Corti sells these teas through a newsletter in two- and four-tael measures (about 2.8 ounces and 5.6 ounces). Supplies are limited since, like wine, vintages sell out.

CRABTREE & EVELYN (R)

1310 Madison Ave. at 93rd St. ❖ 289-3923
520 Madison Ave. bet. 53rd and 54th Sts. ❖ 758-6419
620 Fifth Ave. at Rockefeller Center ❖ 581-5022
151 World Trade Center Concourse ❖ 432-7134
Hours: Hours vary according to location

CRABTREE & EVELYN (MO)

P.O. Box 187; Woodstock Hill, CT 02681 ❖ (860) 928-2761

Crabtree & Evelyn franchised its first owner-operated boutique on Carnegie Hill a few years ago. Since then, the company has expanded to other locations around town. These deliciously scented shops stock more than two dozen teas in charming boxes and must-save tins. Delectables that no self-respecting tea cart should be without include a traditional lemon curd offered in Crabtree & Evelyn's signature octagonal jar—which can be recycled into a juice glass or used to store your homemade preserves. Beautifully illustrated catalogs of comestibles and gifts such as the Tea for Two box and a pricier Banbury Cross Tea Box are available.

THE COFFEE GRINDER (R) (MO)
348 E. 66th St. bet. First and Second Aves.
New York, NY 10021   ❖   (212) 737-3490
Hours: Monday through Friday 9:30 A.M. to 7 P.M.; Saturday
9:30 A.M. to 6 P.M.; closed Sunday

Tucked like a pocket handkerchief between a caterer, a beauty salon, and a low-rise apartment building on a quiet East Side block near New York Hospital, this twenty-year-old shop is outfitted, library-style, with floor-to-ceiling polished pine shelves displaying a wide assortment of coffees and teas, as well as kettles, pots, caddies, and infusers. A chalkboard tots up the myriad offerings, including three dozen loose black teas and a half dozen herbals. Of these, the Russian Georgia, Keemun Congo, and a new plantation—Kenya Michimikuru—stand out. Teas are replenished in five to ten pound increments to ensure freshness. Boxed tea bags include black teas from Jacksons of Piccadilly, Fortnum ⅋ Mason, and Gourmet Ceylon; herbals from Eastern Shore, San Francisco Herb and Natural Food Co., and Health and Heather; tisanes from Pompadour; Bencheley decafs in canisters; Queen's Empire in a handy balsa wood box; and an Uncle Lee green tea. A miscellany of bags is available near hot water for tea-on-the-go, and, in warm weather, a bistro table and chairs are set out on the sidewalk for those who wish to stop and set a spell. Some candies, biscotti, and preserves in Triomphe jars round out the inventory. The Coffee Grinder will make up gift baskets to order, blend custom teas, and set up a schedule whereby regular orders can be shipped weekly.

DAVID LEE HOFFMAN SILK ROAD TEAS (R) (MO)
P.O. Box 287; Lagunitas, CA 94938 ❖ (415) 488-9017

David Lee Hoffman, a wholesale tea importer, owns a tea plantation in China, and has joint ventures with several old-established tea gardens there. His selection of mail-order teas changes frequently, depending upon seasonal offerings. A recent pair of green tea samplers—his specialty—featured twelve top-grade green teas, hand-picked and processed using traditional skills, from the first flush spring harvest. Sampler #1 offered six teas, among them the poetically named Clouds and Mist Lin An. Sampler #2 included Green Peony Rosette and Simao Big Leaf Wild. The exuberant Hoffman can also be found at the Marin County Farmers Market, San Rafael Civic Center, on Thursday and Saturday mornings, from 8 A.M. to 1 P.M., personally selling some of his more than one hundred pure leaf teas—black, oolong, and green—to the public.

DEAN ⊗ DELUCA (R) (MO)
560 Broadway bet. Prince and Spring Sts.
New York, NY 10012 ❖ (212) 431-1691
Hours: Monday through Saturday 10 A.M. to 8 P.M.; Sunday
10 A.M. to 7 P.M.

This emporium of fine foods is revered by anyone who cooks—or pretends to. The selection of teas is the most extensive anywhere. Listing them is an almost intimidating endeavor, but here goes, shelf-by-shelf:

Harney & Sons; Sabbathday Lake Shakers' infusions; The Republic of Tea; Eastern Shore Tea Company's perfumed teas; Grace Rare Teas; Twinings, of course; Jacksons of Piccadilly; Typhoo; Kusmi-Thé; Lyon's Green Label box of fifty bags; Barry's Classic and Gold blends; Fortnum & Mason; Roger Vergé's personal mix; Parisian-based La Tour d'Argent restaurant's private blend; Pompadour tisanes; Sundial Gardens' herbals; Simpson & Vail, represented by two oolongs and an English Breakfast; Mariage Frères; Dr. Stuart's Botanical Tea; Brombertee; Royal Gardens Tea; Drysdale's of Edinburgh in tartan tins; Le Cordon Bleu's special blends; and Rowley's of Ireland. Dean & Deluca also stocks a number of teapots and kettles, including a Russell Hobbs electric and a classic Revere whistler plus sturdy cups and mugs, many oversized. Dean & Deluca maintains eateries at 121 Prince Street, at 75 University Place, in Rockefeller Plaza, and in the Paramount Hotel at 235 West 46th Street. Ditto One Wall Street Court. A mail-order catalog is available, for $2.50, offering a short list of teas.

EMPIRE COFFEE & TEA COMPANY (R) (MO)
592 Ninth Ave. bet. 42nd and 43rd Sts.
New York, NY 10036 ❖ 586-1717; (800) 262-5908
Hours: Weekdays 8 A.M. to 7 P.M.; Saturday 9 A.M. to 6:30 P.M.; Sunday 11 A.M. to 5 P.M.

This no-frills, family-run operation has zigzagged within a five-block radius in Hell's Kitchen since its opening in 1908. It currently resides on Food Row one block north of Port Authority and close to the theater district, so it is a handy stopover for commuters and matinee mavens. Bulk teas number almost six dozen, ranging from blacks to scented flavors. Boxed bags include some originals: Angel Blend Flu-Fighter; Traditional Medicine's American GinZing; Breezy Morning's Nite Cap—for nerves or insomnia—and Uncle Lee's Body Slim Dieter Tea with a tapemeasured waistline illustrated on its box top. Empire sells one kettle and a classic white porcelain pot as well as a few mugs. A catalog and flyer are available.

GOURMET GARAGE (R)

2567 Broadway bet. 96th and 97th Sts. ❖ 663-0656
301 East 64th St. bet. First and Second Aves. ❖ 535-5880
453 Broome St. at Mercer St. ❖ 941-5850
Hours: Monday through Saturday 8 A.M. to 9 P.M.; Sunday
8 A.M. to 8 P.M.

A mecca for fanatical cooks, the Gourmet Garage "garages" a mind-boggling panoply of goodies, both fresh and packaged. In terms of tea, they package their own, under their own name, in convenient little canisters, each of which contains twenty-five bags. Gourmet Garage boasts the standard array of tea: Earl Grey, in zingy and decaf versions, English Breakfast, Darjeeling, Chamomile, Chamomile Mint, and Peppermint, as well as Hibiscus. Our favorite, though, is the one they call Jump Start. Zero to sixty in one minute flat.

GRACE TEA COMPANY, LTD. (MO)
50 W. 17th St.
New York, NY 10011   ❖   (212) 255-2935

Dick and Rita Sanders' personal and long-standing love affair with teas is manifest in their selection of fourteen custom rare teas which include their own Connoisseur Master and Owner's Custom Label favorites. All Grace teas are hand-plucked and hand-blended by their tea tasters on site, as the Sanders' aver, to create simple, basic teas of superb quality. Add to this list three other specialties: Gunpowder Pearl Pinhead green tea and two tisanes, Egyptian Chamomile and Pure Peppermint. All teas are hand-packed in black tins in both half-pound and two-ounce sampler sizes. Three teas—the Winey Keemun, the Earl Grey mixture, and the Connoisseur—also come bagged in boxes of fifty. For New Yorkers, Grace teas can be found at Dean ❧ Deluca and at Grace's on Third Avenue at 71st Street, among other locations.

GRACE'S MARKETPLACE (R)
1237 Third Ave. at 71st St.   ❖   737-0600
Hours: Monday through Saturday 7 A.M. to 8:30 P.M.; Sunday
8 A.M. to 7 P.M.

The tea section of this always-crowded Upper East Side fine foods emporium is slightly overwhelmed by the cafes, but not to worry, you will find a nice selection of bagged teas here, some of which are unique to this store. To whit: Whittard of Chelsea; Sushi Chef green tea; Alyssa fruit tea; and Barrow's American Breakfast. Other stand-bys are Grace Rare Teas, Dr. Stuart's tisanes, and herbals from Stash, the London Herb & Spice Company, The Republic of Tea, and Celestial Seasonings. Bigelow Premium is here as is Twinings. Wagner's is represented by decafs. Check out the go-withs while you are at it, too, such as the bakery goods, honeys, and preserves.

HARNEY & SONS, LTD. (R) (MO)
Village Green; P.O. Box 676
Salisbury, CT 06068 ❖ (800) TEA-TIME
Hours: Daily 9 A.M. to 5 P.M.

The Harneys—father John, son Michael—supply quality tea to many of New York City's grand hotels and posh department stores. Their tea bags are particularly good since they are packed with small leaves, not fannings. The extensive gourmet section of the reader-friendly mail order catalog offers a second flush Darjeeling from the Namring garden and a Nilgiri black tea from Southern India, noted for its mellow round flavor. There are books and a section on tea gift packages includes "What Does the Future Hold?" This is comprised of Harney & Sons' *Tea Leaf Reading* book, an official tea leaf reading cup, a 3-ounce tin of Orange Pekoe, and provisions for your table—jam, honey, etc. The teaware includes Yixing, English hotel silver, and Ritz-Carlton teapots. You can also buy from the office store.

IMPERIAL TEA COURT (R) (MO)
1411 Powell St.
San Francisco, CA 94133 ❖ (415) 788-6080

In 1993, in conjunction with the American Tea Masters Association, a private society of tea connoisseurs, Imperial Tea Court tea merchants first offered for sale the top one hundred prize-winning green teas of the China National Tea Rating Awards. The names make for delightful reading—Star Shadows on Celestial Lake of Jade Bamboo, for instance, and The Valiant Canary, Song of the Ivory Butterfly, and Portal of the Elder Swallow. These can now be bought at the store each year. The Imperial Tea Court mail order catalog changes frequently according to seasonal availabilities, but generally sixty to one hundred primarily green teas are offered. You can also request the James Norwood Pratt Tea Luxuries catalog of tea and utensils; the latter includes a jade 'guywan' (traditional lidded cup).

JEFFERSON MARKET (R)
450 Sixth Ave. bet. 10th and 11th Sts. ❖ 675-2277
Hours: Monday through Saturday 8 A.M. to 9 P.M.; Sunday 9 A.M. to 8 P.M.

Since 1929 Jefferson Market has been selling top-of-the-line foodstuffs right beside the everyday necessities in a friendly, small-town environment where no item—or question—is too big or too small for this local treasure's attention. With its recent move, across the street, into larger quarters (formerly the home of a bank and dry cleaner), tea (and coffee) takes center stage right at the entrance. There's a wide selection of beautifully packaged Harney's tea, both loose in tins and 25 bags in a gift-like bag, plus virtually all of our old-fashioned favorites. There's even the occasional tea-tasting here.

THOMAS J. LIPTON (MO)
800 Sylvan Ave.
Englewood Cliffs, NJ 07632 ❖ (800) 697-7887

Established by the entrepreneur yachtsman, Sir Thomas Lipton, in 1898, Lipton is now America's biggest tea vendor; no less than forty million of the company's tea bags are brewed daily. However, many Lipton lovers are frustrated that their local supermarkets do not have the shelf space to consistently stock a preferred blend or brew. While Lipton does not have a catalog, the good news is that you can order any one of their teas, including national favorites such as Mountainberry Apple, Lemon Soother, Lipton's Green Tea, and Iced Tea mixes, like Peach and Raspberry, by using the company's toll-free number listed above.

MYERS OF KESWICK (R)

634 Hudson St. bet. Horatio and Jane Sts. ❖ 691-4194

Hours: Monday through Friday 10 A.M. to 7 P.M.; Saturday 10 A.M. to 6 P.M.; Sunday Noon to 5 P.M.

Keswick is a town in the English Lake District, and that is where Mr. Myers himself comes from. His capacious wood-floored store is the kind of genial, down-to-earth grocers store that is not so easy to find even in England anymore. Its decor depends on the shopkeeper's pride and glory of meticulously tidy shelves of homey provender, not the phony kind like Gentlemens Relish. Come Christmas, Myer's, always lively, is thronged with the nostalgia-prone who just cannot go on any longer without their Smarties, McVities' Chocolate Digestives, Twiglets, thick rashers of British bacon, and Cumberland sausages. Date-stamped English Typhoo, Lyons, and P.G. Tips are also available. These are the teas that got the British through the blitz: they brew up fast and strong, and are drunk with milk and plenty of sugar. Churchill drank gallons in the Whitehall War Room. Mr. Myers makes the lemon curd tarts, eccles cakes, pork pies, and bangers himself. In winter there are fruit cakes by Bryson Gold Medal Bakers in Keswick, and Bell's of Lazonby. Do not miss the tea cozies hand-knit by the owner's mother in British football club colors.

NEW WAH YIN HONG ENTERPRISES (R)
232 Canal St. bet. Centre and Baxter Sts.   ❖   226-2390
Hours: Daily 10 A.M. to 8:30 P.M.

You may feel like a salmon trying to get upriver in this frequently crowded, compact Chinatown supermarket. Squeeze past the customers who are buying traditional herbal remedies at the counter to find the teas located on their shelves in the back of the left-hand aisle. Many of them are produced by the Shanghai and Guangdong Tea branches of the China National Native Produce and Animal By-Products Corporation. The teas are robust and flavorful—the Keemun has a strong fragrance and powerfully winey character. You could almost make the black rose tea into potpourri sachets. As the perfumed petals unfurl in water, they release the scent of distant Chinese gardens. Colorfully decorated tins of vanilla and fruited black teas are imported by American Roland Corporation. New Wah Yin Hong also sells green and oolong teas, and tea in brick form.

OREN'S DAILY ROAST (R)

1574 First Ave. bet. 81st and 82nd Sts. ❖ 737-2690

1144 Lexington Ave. bet. 79th and 80th Sts. ❖ 472-6830

33 E. 58th St. bet. Madison and Park Aves. ❖ 838-3345

434 Third Ave. bet. 30th and 31st Sts. ❖ 779-1241

Hours: Monday through Friday 7 A.M. to 8 P.M.; Saturday 10 A.M. to 6 P.M.; Sunday 11 A.M. to 6 P.M.

Like a friendly Labrador, the aromatic blast of roasting coffee almost knocks you over as you approach. While it is true "coffee is the heart of Oren's" there are seventeen black, oolong, flavored, and decaf loose teas for sale in the four New York City stores, safely kept in airtight glass jars. Packaged teas are represented by Republic of Tea offerings, and the new Ferris & Roberts fruit- and flower-flavored herbal infusions. The Lexington Avenue store also has a nice selection of books from serious to lighthearted, greeting and note cards, and a selection of useful tea utensils such as the sturdy Watson Safari teapot; this British import is made from terra-cotta stamped with a droll inscription. This Oren's carries about twelve functional teapot styles, and some twenty collectable novelty teapots.

PORTO RICO IMPORTING COMPANY (R)

201 Bleecker St. bet. Sixth Ave. and McDougal St. ❖ 477-5421
40½ St. Mark's Pl. bet. First and Second Aves. ❖ 533-1982
Hours: Monday through Saturday 9 A.M. to 9 P.M.; Sunday
Noon to 7 P.M.

With its back-to-basics decor and no-nonsense service, Porto Rico
delivers what it promises—more than six dozen loose leaf teas of every
type, displayed in weighty glass jars, as well as coffee beans in burlap
bags. To witness the daily lineup, it is the quality of tea (and, of
course, coffee) that counts here, not pinkie finger-in-the-air niceties.
The few accoutrements set out along the opposite wall from the
bustling weighing counter and cash register appear almost as an aside
rather than a carefully tended-to buyer's dream. The stainless steel
kettles, in four sizes, for instance, are sturdy, serviceable numbers with
no pretense to design; they range from $15.98 to $27.98. Porto Rico
sells a standard selection of bagged teas, too, including some from
Twinings and Bencheley. The St. Mark's Place store is a smaller version of its Bleecker Street counterpart.

REPUBLIC OF TEA (MO)
8 Digital Dr., Suite 100
Novato, CA 94949 ❖ (800) 354-5530

As the Minister of Leaves whimsically observes in The Republic of Tea's *TeaMind Times*, "Tea is contentment. Contentment is love of content. Drinking tea, desires diminish and I come to see the ancient secret of happiness: wanting what I already have, inhabiting the life that is already mine." Read on for more insights from the genial administrators of the mystical republic, such as the Minister of Propaganda, the Minister of Fire and Water, and the Minister of Pots. All this makes for gently humorous reading over what else, but a good cup of tea. The Republic of Tea offers twenty-four leaf, black, oolong, green, and herbal teas, bag teas (such as Organic Breakfast, Mango Ceylon Decaf), and a variety of tea things to use (infuser mug, black iron teapot), and wear (baseball cap, Republic of Tea shirt). Phone for information on seasonal teas offered in small quantities.

THE TEA CLUB   (MO)
1715 North Burling St., Chicago, IL 60614
(800) FULL-LEAF

For the price of membership, the Tea Club sends two tea selections each month: two traditional black, green or oolong teas, or two herbals—or a combination of both. Teas to be offered each month are described in advance. Like a book club, a selection may be replaced or cancelled in a given month. Tea Club gift boxes are also available. Call to learn more about its teas, and for its membership fees.

TEN REN TEA AND GINSENG COMPANY (R) (MO)
75 Mott St. bet. Bayard and Elizabeth Sts.
New York, NY 10013   ❖   349-2286
Hours: Daily 10 A.M. to 8 P.M.

Should it be Ti Kuan Yin Tea, Pu-Erh, or Osmanthus Oolong Tea? Or perhaps Tipsy Poet or Tipsy Beauty Tea? Ordering from the Ten Ren Tea and Ginseng Company catalog presents you with many options over which to ponder. Perhaps some of the black tea or Oolong-flavored candies? The glossy little mail-order catalog is laid out with the same efficient precision displayed by the Mott Street store. The tea itself, sold loose, in tea bags, or in tins, comes in packaging decorated with depictions of Chinese sages, demure goddesses, and tea maidens, bold calligraphy, and lashings of red and gold as festive as Chinese New Year. Do not overlook the Ginseng Oolong King's Tea, reputedly one of the finer teas Ten Ren sells by mail. The wood-boxed Jasmine, Oolong, Ti Kuan Yin, or mixed tea bag sampler makes a nice small gift. Ten Ren also offers American-grown ginseng, both wild and cultivated, as tea or in capsules.

UPTON TEA IMPORTS (MO)

P.O. Box 159; Upton, MA 01568
Orders: (800) 234-8327; Inquiries: (508) 529-6299
Hours: Monday through Friday 9 A.M. to 5 P.M.; Saturday
9 A.M. to 3 P.M.

As a teenager, Tom Eck loved tea so much he used to send to England for it. As a much-traveled computer expert, he made a point of visiting Taiwan's tea shops and gardens. In England and France he got to know professional tea tasters and prestige tea merchants. These relationships served him well when, five years ago, Eck started his company. A true tea connoisseur, Eck approaches a tea's seasonal, climatic, and regional character with thoughtful consideration. The close to one hundred and thirty black, oolong, and green flavored teas and decaffeinated teas in his mail-order catalog are concisely but effectively characterized. His teas hail from India, Nepal, Sri Lanka, China, Japan, and Africa. Eck often buys small lots; for example, he will take two chests of a garden's total production of four. The newsletter/catalog is available four times a year, and through it he also sells teaware such as the Chatsford Teapot, preferred by loose-tea fanciers for its ample drop-in/lift-out infuser.

ZABAR'S (R)

2245 Broadway bet. 80th and 81st Sts.   ❖   787-2000

Hours: Monday through Friday 8 A.M. to 7:30 P.M.; Saturday 8 A.M. to 10 P.M.; Sunday 9 A.M. to 6 P.M.

Generations of New Yorkers have grown up with Zabar's as the place to go for wonderful cheeses, great deli foodstuffs, baked goods, and prepared foods at low prices. Exotic imported foods overpopulate the miles of shelves, and there is an ever-seething conga line of hungry foodies to be found snaking their way through Zabar's congested aisles. Upstairs you can find everything for the practical kitchen, along with good basic teaware like the Jena 'Museum' glass teapot. On the street level, the tea enclave hosts some lofty and some lesser known brands. The savings make it worthwhile to take a cab home with your shopping bags. Load up on sumptuous imported preserves for the tea table, clotted cream, cookies, and cakes while you're at it.

About Tea

The Legendary Origins of Tea

Tea, it is said, was discovered in China in 2737 B.C., by Emperor Shen Nong. Attentive to matters of health and hygiene, the emperor was fastidious in such practices as boiling water. On one occasion, as he stoked the fire under his kettle, he plucked branches from a shrub close at hand and tossed them into the flames. A few leaves floated, by accident, into the water. As the leaves colored the water, the emperor, marveling at the fragrance that arose from the smoke, sipped the brew that resulted. Captivated both by its flavor and by the stimulating feelings it generated, he hastened to advocate "ch'a," or tea, as an antidote for a plethora of ills from indigestion to lethargy.

Almost ten centuries later, poet Lu Yu wrote about the ceremony that had evolved around the preparation and presentation of tea. In his renowned *Book of Tea*, the poet described how the ritual mirrored an inward ethic which embraced respect and courtesy. Within this small, simple, generous—and beautiful—act, a harmony between host and guest could be realized, a harmony underlying all of life. Tea was a work of art.

A Short Glossary of Teas

The following are some of the teas that are served, both loose and in bags, at the various New York venues. The ubiquitous Orange Pekoe is named for a grade of tea, not for a varietal. Some teas are exclusive to their makers: Lady Londonderry, a strong Ceylon/India/China blend from Jacksons of Piccadilly; Black Currant, a fruity blend, and Prince of Wales, an aromatic blend of China teas, both from Twinings.

TEA	COUNTRY OF ORIGIN	TYPE	TASTE
Assam	India	Varietal	Bright, hearty, malty
Ceylon	Sri Lanka	Varietal	Light, mellow, pungent, with a golden hue
Darjeeling, the "champagne of teas"	India	Varietal	Light, delicate, flowery, full-bodied, with an amber hue
Keemun, the "burgundy of teas"	China	Varietal	Sweet, flowery, full-bodied, with a deep amber hue
Lapsang/ Souchong	China	Varietal	Distinctive, smoky flavor
English Breakfast	Ceylon/ India	Blend	Rich, brisk, medium-bodied
Irish Breakfast	Ceylon/ India	Blend	Stronger than English Breakfast, pungent, full-bodied

(continued)

TEA	COUNTRY OF ORIGIN	TYPE	TASTE
Russian Caravan	❖	Blend	Robust, smoky
Earl Grey	China/ India	Blend	Scented, flavored with oil of bergamot (a citrus fruit)
Jasmine	❖	❖	Scented, fragrant, mild, delicate
Formosa/ Oolong	Taiwan	Oolong	Aromatic, flowery, without astringency
Gunpowder	Taiwan/ China	Green	Penetrating, often slightly bitter, mildly astringent, yellow-green in hue
Chamomile	❖	Herbal	Flowery, soothing
Rose hips	❖	Herbal	Tart, fruity, astringent

Storing Tea

When you purchase loose leaf tea by the ounce, transfer it as soon as possible to an opaque container such as an airtight tin, or a tea caddy, and store it in a cupboard; your tea should stay fresh for months. Tea fades when exposed to light, so do not keep it in a glass container. Tea is adversely affected by moisture, so it should not be refrigerated or frozen. Tea bags should also be kept free of moisture and away from light, so if you transfer them from the box in which they were purchased, make sure they are stored in a similar manner as loose leaf tea.

How to Make a Cup of Black Tea

1. Fill a kettle with cold water. (Cold water contains more oxygen than hot water; it is the oxygen that creates bubbles in the water to cause furled tea leaves to open and release their flavor.)

2. Bring water to the rolling boil for black tea. Do not overboil. (Overboiling causes the water to lose oxygen and can make the tea taste muddy.) *Do not underboil.* (Underboiling results in a thin tea that is both tasteless and tepid.)

3. While the water is coming to the boil, run hot water into the teapot. Swirl the water in the teapot, or let it sit for 2 minutes; pour out. The warmth of the pot will allow the dry tea leaves to begin to relax in anticipation of their immersion in the boiling water.

4. To the teapot, add one heaping teaspoon of loose tea for each cup. Do not use a teaball or infuser, if possible, as these confine the leaves.

5. Bring the teapot to the kettle, not vice versa. Every moment counts when preparing a cup of tea!

6. Pour the boiling water over tea leaves in the teapot. Let the tea steep for 3 to 5 minutes. Leaves will double in size as they steep. Brewing times vary, so consult your tea tin for recommended optimum time. (Overbrewing will cause the tea to stew and turn bitter.) Stir the tea gently after brewing.

7. Pour small amount of the tea through a strainer and into a cup. Dilute to taste with hot, boiled water. Add milk, if desired, or lemon. M.I.F.–Milk In First–was instigated to ensure that a fragile porcelain cup would not break when boiling water was poured into it. These days, you can add your milk before, or after, as you wish. Milk cuts the astringency of the tannin in tea. The addition of lemon originated in Russia. Take your pick. Or, drink tea neat as the purists do.

Black teas taste bitter after sitting in the pot too long, so they should be discarded after a single pour. (Oolong teas may be infused more than once; in fact, the Chinese believe that subsequent infusions–up to seven–bring increasing amounts of luck.)

After tea, the pot need only be rinsed. Soap or detergent can leave a residue that will affect subsequent pours. And then, feed your leaves to a compost pile, if you can.

How to Make a Cup of Green Tea

1. Bring warm water just barely to the boiling point; the water should be piping hot, but not actually boiling. (Green tea leaves are very delicate and the action of the bursting bubbles of a rolling boil is too violent for them.)

2. Place a teaspoon or two of the leaves in a pot, pour hot water over leaves, and let steep for just a minute, or less. Pour into cup.

Index by Neighborhood

CENTRAL VILLAGE/GRAMERCY

ABC Carpet & Home   64

Barnes & Noble Cafe   23

Fishs Eddy   74

Lady Mendl's Tea Salon   13

Oren's Daily Roast   102

Parlour Cafe at ABC Carpet & Home   49

Pier 1 Imports   82

T Salon & Tea Emporium   35

William-Wayne & Company   85

CHELSEA

Barnes & Noble Cafe   23

EAST MIDTOWN

The Astor Court at the St. Regis   6

Barnes & Noble Cafe   23

Bernardaud   70

Cafe SFA at Saks Fifth Avenue   48

Cardel   72

The Cocktail Terrace at the Waldorf-Astoria   7

Crabtree & Evelyn   91

Fitzers at the Fitzpatrick   8

Fortunoff   75

The Garden Cafe at the Hotel Kitano   10

The Gotham Lounge at the Peninsula   11

Istana at the New York Palace   12

James II Galleries Ltd.   77

James Robinson   78

The Lobby Lounge at the Four Seasons   16

MacKenzie-Childs Ltd.   30, 80

The Morgan Court at the Pierpont Morgan Library   54

115

UPPER WEST SIDE

About the Authors

BO NILES is an editor and writer who specializes in design and decoration. She is a contributing editor to *Country Living* magazine and the author of a number of books including *White by Design* and *Living with Lace*. Her collection of teaware includes her great-grandmother's silver tea service, four pink lusterware teacups, and a mug from the Pussy Willow Tea Room in Glasgow, Scotland.

VERONICA McNIFF is an arts administrator and freelance writer specializing in the decorative arts. Her articles are published in magazines such as *House Beautiful* and *Travel & Leisure*. She collects royal commemorabilia teaware—some of which she uses at her yearly Boxing Day Tea.

About the Illustrator

SUSAN COLGAN is a painter whose still lifes are published in *Among Flowers*, a collaboration with poet Susan Kinsolving. She lives and works in New York and Berkshire County, Massachusetts.